SPATIAL ASPECTS OF AGING

Robert F. Wiseman
University of Kansas

RESOURCE PAPERS FOR COLLEGE GEOGRAPHY NO. 78-4

Copyright 1978
by the
Association of American Geographers
1710 Sixteenth Street, N.W.
Washington, D. C. 20009

Library of Congress Card Number 78-59103
ISBN 0-89291-133-6

FOREWORD

In 1968, the Commission on College Geography of the Association of American Geographers published its first Resource Paper, *Theories of Urban Location,* by Brian J. L. Berry. In 1974, coinciding with the termination of NSF funding for the Commission, Resource Paper number 28 appeared, *The Underdevelopment and Modernization of the Third World,* by Anthony R. deSouza and Philip W. Porter. Of the many CCG activities, the Resource Papers Series became an effective means for permitting both teachers and students to keep abreast of developments in the field.

Because of the popularity and usefulness of the Resource Papers, the AAG applied for and received a two-year grant from NSF to continue to produce Resource Papers and to put the series on a self-supporting basis. The 1977 Series was the first group produced entirely with AAG funding.

In an effort to increase the utility of these papers, the Resource Papers Panel has attempted to be particularly sensitive to the currency of materials for undergraduate geography courses and to the writing style of these papers. The present Panel continues to affirm the original purposes of the Series, which are quoted below:

> The Resource Papers have been developed as expository documents for the use of both the student and the instructor. They are experimental in that they are designed to supplement existing texts and to fill a gap between significant research in American geography and readily accessible materials. The papers are concerned with important concepts or topics in modern geography and focus on one of three general themes: geographic theory; policy implications; or contemporary social relevance. They are designed to complement a variety of undergraduate college geography courses at the introductory and advanced level.

The Resource Papers are developed, printed, and distributed under the auspices of the Association of American Geographers. The ideas presented in these papers do not imply endorsement by the AAG.

Many individuals have assisted in producing these Resource Papers, and we wish to acknowledge those who assisted the Panel in reviewing the authors' prospectuses, in reading and commenting on the various drafts, and in making helpful suggestions. The Panel also acknowledges the perceptive suggestions and editorial assistance of Jane F. Castner and Teresa A. Mulloy of the AAG Central Office.

Salvatore J. Natoli
Association of American Geographers
Editor, Resource Papers Series

Resource Papers Panel:

John F. Lounsbury, Arizona State University
Mark S. Monmonier, Syracuse University
Harold A. Winters, Michigan State University

EDITOR'S NOTE

With the publication of *Spatial Aspects of Aging*, my tenure as editor of the Resource Papers Series ends. The series now numbers sixteen papers covering the geographical aspects and issues related to land use controls, suburbanization, the world food problem, maps and their meaning, international tourism, transportation, landscape in literature, mental health, environmental quality, migration patterns, school desegregation, energy, crime and violence, water resources, environmental impact statements, and the aging. It is an eclectic list and for the most part represents the broad spectrum of societal issues that can be illuminated, ameliorated, and perhaps even resolved by our paying closer attention to the contributions geographical research, study, and analysis can make in today's world.

This series has elaborated on and built upon the strong foundations and precedents set by the original Resource Papers Series that began in 1968 under the aegis of the AAG's Commission on College Geography. We estimate that during the past decade over 400,000 Resource Papers found their way into college classrooms and indeed fulfilled their basic purpose to enrich the undergraduate course offerings in college geography. These forty-four papers are a testimony to the AAG's continuing commitment to enhancing geographic education. Also gratifying has been the positive response we received from geographers in non-academic positions as well as professionals in other disciplines.

A retiring editor can indulge in some personal recollections and can look back over the past five years with both pleasure and pain. Fortunately the pleasures and rewards have outweighed the pains, and many of the pains have been labor pains that eventually delivered vigorous offspring. The pleasurable occasions included working with my colleagues on the Resource Papers Panel whose selfless, highly professional, and intellectual contributions smoothed out the many rough spots. The series would not have been possible without their continuing counsel, steady support, and commitment. John F. Lounsbury of Arizona State, Mark S. Monmonier of Syracuse, and Harold A. Winters of Michigan State are all professionals and men of good will and humor. They helped sort through dozens of proposals and offered valued critical advice. They also gently twisted arms along the way when some of the work fell behind schedule, and Mark, in particular, speeded up a deadline by a year by completing a paper to fill a spot when an author withdrew at the last minute. The many reviewers of proposals and manuscripts served with dedication and helped to enhance and maintain the quality of the series. The authors themselves, to a person retained their equanimity and good spirits when the editor's blue pencil not infrequently got carried away. They are indeed an outstanding group of geographers. We all learned a great deal from and about each other. Finally, but not the least of all are Jane F. Castner, formerly of the AAG Central Office and now at Rutgers Law School, who made certain that everything was ready for the printer and served as an excellent non-geographical reader of manuscripts to insure clarity of writing and logic of exposition and Teresa Mulloy, the current editorial assistant, who performed the same role on the last two papers.

Because my eyes were the last to see the manuscripts, any imperfections that have persisted can be credited exclusively to me.

Salvatore J. Natoli
Washington, D. C.
March 1979

PREFACE

Growing concern for the elderly segment of society has resulted in the development of a burgeoning literature on aging and a proliferation of aging courses throughout the social sciences. To a large extent this is because of a recent recognition of the many problems confronting older Americans. However, the study of aging takes on even broader significance when we realize that America, like other modern nations, is an aging society. Each year the elderly population increases relative to other age groups.

Geographers are increasingly focusing research on older people and have already made significant contributions to this growing body of knowledge. As is the case with any emerging area of study, the geographical literature is scattered across many specific topics, and the focal points of study which will ultimately structure this field have not been clearly identified. There is a clear need for articulating the spatial aspects of aging which have received most attention; and for bringing together in an organized fashion the geographic literature in this field. This Resource Paper addresses these needs and began as an attempt to review state-of-the-art knowledge on the geography of older Americans. Soon it became apparent that cognate work in other disciplines must be included and that, even with this supplementary material, large gaps remain in our knowledge of several spatial aspects of aging. Thus, the final Paper that emerged is as much a call for further study as it is an encapsulation of what we already know.

In the next few years our knowledge will expand well beyond what is presented here. Many of the gaps will be filled in and several spatial aspects of aging not recognized in this Paper may emerge ultimately as the most salient dimensions of the field. I hope this Paper will foster further development of this important area of geographic study.

I would like to thank the many geographers who shared the results of their studies and apologize to those whose work eluded my attention. The following people contributed substantially to this Paper by critiquing early drafts: John Augelli, Stephen Golant, Douglas McKelvey, Valerie Preston, Graham Rowles, and Curtis C. Roseman. I thank Laura Poracsky for her cartographic work and Sandy Gilliland for many patient hours of transcription and typing. Finally, special thanks are due Linna Place, Donna Schafer, and Janet Price for their constant encouragement as well as their assistance with library research and the preparation of early drafts.

Robert F. Wiseman
University of Kansas
December, 1978

SUGGESTIONS FOR CLASS USE

The purpose of this Paper is to introduce geography students to the study of aging by describing methodological issues, contemporary theoretical views, and by organizing and reviewing much of the relevant geographical literature. Throughout the paper we will raise important and unanswered research questions. These can provide the bases for class discussion or actual investigation. These questions and the presentation of future aspects of aging found in the last chapter should challenge students to become involved personally in the study of older people and aging.

Teachers and students can use this Paper in modular fashion for human geography courses that consider minority groups and contemporary social issues. Similarly it can be helpful in sociology, urban planning and social gerontology courses because of the wide range of topics it encompasses. Each of these topics, as well as the many spatial aspects of aging that are not fully developed here, could occupy the scope of a paper such as this. The true breadth and depth of each topic can be appreciated only by reading much of the literature referenced in each chapter. Thus, for courses devoted entirely to the geography of older people and aging, it is essential to study this literature carefully. Primarily the Paper has been designed as a point of departure for a more penetrating study of and as a framework for organizing the spatial aspects of aging.

In all classroom uses of this Paper it is important to recognize that the study of aging is truly interdisciplinary. Much of the gerontological literature being developed by other social science disciplines can be adapted to the geography classroom, just as knowledge about the spatial aspects of aging can enrich courses outside of geography.

CONTENTS

	PREFACE	v
	SUGGESTIONS FOR CLASS USE	vi
I.	GEOGRAPHY AND OLDER PEOPLE	1
	Increasing Awareness of Older Americans	1
	Stereotypes Out of Focus	2
	The Study of Aging	3
II.	THEORETICAL PERSPECTIVES ON AGING	5
	Developmental Perspective	5
	Social Theories of Aging	7
	Employing the Multidimensional-Developmental Perspective	8
III.	SPATIAL PATTERNS OF OLDER AMERICANS	9
	Growth of the Elderly Population	9
	National Pattern of Concentration	11
	Urban Concentrations	11
	Processes Producing Elderly Concentrations	17
IV.	ELDERLY MIGRATION	18
	Mobility Rates	18
	National Patterns of Elderly Migration	18
	Local Patterns of Residential Change	21
	A Model of Residential Change	22
V.	ENVIRONMENT AND AGING	24
	Definitions and Dimensions of Environment	24
	Geographical Perspective of Aging Environment Relationships (AER)	25
	Aging Studies of Spatial Interaction	27
	Other Perspectives of AER	28
	Further Geographic Study of AER	30
VI.	ASSISTANCE AND SERVICE DELIVERY	31
	The Service Delivery System	31
	Transportation Services	32
	The Location of Services	34
	A New Program for Meeting Old Needs	35
VII.	"WILL YOU STILL LOVE ME WHEN I'M SIXTY-FOUR?"	36
	The Aging of Society	36
	Changing Characteristics of Older People	37
	Future Study of Aging	38
	BIBLIOGRAPHY	39
	Further Readings	42

LIST OF FIGURES

1.	Percent of the Total Population in the Older Ages: 1900–2040	3
2.	Selected Dimensions of Life Cycle	6
3.	Health Declines with Increasing Age	6
4.	Major Theories of Social Gerontology	8
5.	Age–Sex Population Pyramids for the United States	10
6.	Percent of State Population Age 65 and Over, 1910–1970	14
7.	Counties Experiencing a Large Increase in Percentage of Elderly People, 1950–1970	15
8.	Distribution of Elderly in Wichita, Kansas	16
9.	Mobility Rates Over the Life Span	19
10.	Mobility Rates for Select Cohorts of U.S. Population, 1975–1976	20
11.	U.S. Interstate Migration of Persons Age 60 and Over, 1965–1970	21
12.	Theoretical Model of Elderly Migration Process	23
13.	Environmental Spaces and Levels of Action	26
14.	Schematic Portrayal of Age-Loss Continuum Across the Life Span	28
15.	Schematic Representation of an Ecological Model of Aging	29
16.	Relative Satisfaction of the Elderly with the Distance from Their Building to Necessary Facilities	35

LIST OF TABLES

1.	The Age-Loss Continuum	7
2.	U.S. Population Age 65 and Over, 1900–2000	9
3.	Increases in Average Life Span Remaining	11
4.	U.S. Population Age 65 and Over, 1976	12
5.	Percent of U.S. Population Age 65 and Over, 1910–1970	13
6.	Comparison of Activities Within the Past Year	27
7.	Per Capita Trips per Week	33

I. GEOGRAPHY AND OLDER PEOPLE

What does life hold in store after the retirement banquet? What does one think about when one winds and places the gold watch on the dresser? Are thoughts of the future intermingled with warm reminiscences of the past? Does one look forward to the next twenty years with pleasant anticipation or with trepidation? Twenty million Americans are living the answers to these questions. Most of us will one day confront these questions. How will we respond? Will we be much different from our grandparents? Although most of us will probably avoid these questions for many years, thinking about them now provides a good starting point for considering older people, their life experiences, their problems, and society's response to those problems.

Geographers are increasingly devoting attention to the study of older people. This is appropriate because many of the problems of later life and many of the contemporary issues of social gerontology have important spatial components. For example, need assessment surveys of the elderly reveal that many older people experience transportation problems such as difficulties in getting to the store, visiting friends, and traveling to the doctor's office. For a variety of reasons many no longer have an automobile, some have physical impairments which make even walking difficult, and for some public mass transit is not available. Clearly their spatial mobility is limited resulting in obvious hardship. This problem is exacerbated by the spatial structure of today's urban environments, e.g., recent decentralization of retailing and service functions from the Central Business District (CBD) to suburban locations and the demise of neighborhood shopping activities. Thus, at a time when the environment demands greater geographical mobility than ever before just to sustain life, many older people have less mobility than they did earlier in life.

Another example of the relevance of geography to the study of older people can be found in the planning and development of service delivery programs designed to meet the needs of the elderly. Where are those older people most in need located? How does demand for special services vary across space? How important are distance and accessibility to the use of services provided? How are service systems to be configured spatially? These are important questions to service providers and ultimately to the quality of life experienced by older people.

In these and other areas geographers are making important contributions to our understanding of older people. The primary purpose of this Resource Paper is to review many of those contributions, articulate areas where geographical inquiry is developing, and to identify issues that require further geographical study. But, the results of studying older people need not be limited solely to geographers contributing to social gerontology while receiving little in return. Study of the aged leads inexorably to the study of aging, the processes of change throughout life. Considering aging over the entire life span calls attention to the fact that we base much of our geographical understanding of human behavior upon a static view of life. Our models often ignore the vast differences among various age groups and even among the different stages of life experienced by any individual. To the extent that geographers consider the broader implications of aging as they study the aged, the discipline of geography will be enriched.

Although we could examine numerous spatial aspects of aging, a few are emerging as focal points for growing bodies of geographical literature on older people. Each chapter in this paper addresses one of these aspects. The first, presented in Chapter III, deals with the spatial distribution of the U.S. elderly population as it has evolved over time. Fundamental questions include: Where do we find older people? Are there distinctive concentrations that form discernible patterns? Why do these patterns exist and how are they changing? The second aspect, presented in Chapter IV, focuses upon spatial patterns of elderly migration and addresses questions such as, where are older people moving to and from, and how does this movement influence the distributional pattern of older people? We will also discuss the processes responsible for elderly migration. Chapter V considers a third aspect, the nature of relationships that exist between the older individual and the environment, the ways in which the individual geographically experiences the environment, and how the environmental setting affects the life of an older person. A final aspect, presented in Chapter VI, is that of geographic research applied to the planning of service delivery systems, housing, and other programs designed to assist older people.

The context surrounding geographical study of aging also warrants attention. The remainder of this chapter describes the growing general concern for older people, commonly held stereotypes, and the ways in which researchers examine aging and older people. Chapter II discusses prevailing paradigmatic and theoretical views of aging as they are relevant to geographical study. After considering the spatial aspects of aging, Chapter VII addresses the future, especially the future conditions of older people. This is important in our own lives because we will one day join this group, but more importantly, it is highly relevant today in planning the future of our aging society.

Increasing Awareness of Older Americans

Never before has America been so concerned about the welfare of its senior citizens. During the past 10 years the federal government has enacted more special programs to benefit older people than in all the previous decades combined. These new programs reflect governmental concern for providing income through social security and supplemental security income payments; tax benefits, such as extra exemptions on income tax forms and relief from local property tax in some communities; Medicare and Medicaid; senior centers; Meals on Wheels; congregate meals, a "hot-lunch program;" limited home repair and maintenance; homemaker services; and even specially designed transportation systems.

The popular media regularly feature stories that present some of the problems of older people. Who can forget stories about the old woman who eats cat food because she cannot afford to buy other kinds of meat? Such stories, although true, reflect the life experiences of only a very few older Americans. Still, these and less sensational stories of older people reflect society's increasing awareness of its senior citizens.

Concern for older people is not likely to diminish in the future, for the United States, like many developed countries, is an aging society. That is, the elderly segments of society are growing faster than other age groups. Figure 1 depicts the U.S. trend since the beginning of this century and shows government forecasts to the year 2040, a time when most of us will be old. At that time it is likely that nearly one out of every five citizens will be classified as elderly!

There are many reasons for recognizing the problems confronting older Americans. Although the elderly comprise approximately 10 percent of the U.S. population they include 20 percent of those Americans with incomes below official poverty levels; in 1974, median annual income for those older people not living with relatives was only $2,950. Nearly 20 percent have health problems that limit their mobility; over 75 percent suffer one or more chronic health conditions. More than half of all women age 65 and older are widows and this increases to almost 70 percent of all women age 75 or more. The prospect of remarriage after widowhood is very low when one considers that in 1977 widows outnumbered widowers by 5.2 to 1. In the same year over six million persons age 65 and over, or 41.7 percent of the elderly population were living alone, an increase of 27.8 percent since 1970. These and other statistics describe old age as a time of loneliness, poor health and poverty; a time when problems are numerous and the individual's resources for dealing with problems have reached a lifetime low. These statistics support the popular image of aging expressed by the Beatles singing "Will you still need me, will you still feed me when I'm 64?" or Simon and Garfunkel poignantly admonishing us to "Say hello in there, hello."

Stereotypes Out of Focus

In light of the above statistics, it is not surprising that society holds a negative perception of old age. Much of this negative perception is based upon inaccurate stereotypes. Even more unfortunate is that most older people embrace these stereotypes while viewing themselves as exceptions. A 1975 national study provided many examples that dramatically illustrate this situation (Harris and Associates, 1975). For every older person who feels that life is now worse than what they thought it would be, there are three who say it is better. Fifty-one percent of the general public believe that "poor health" is a severe problem for the aged individual whereas only 21 percent of older people reported it as a personal problem. "Not having enough money to live on" was thought to be a significant problem by 62 percent of the public but only 15 percent of the elderly said it was. Over 60 percent of the public believe that old people spend a great deal of time watching television and just "sitting and thinking" although only 30 percent of the elderly actually do. Just five percent of the public felt that older people are "very active sexually," but 16 percent of the older males and seven percent of the females said they are. These figures are surprisingly high when they are related to sex ratios and the large number of older people living alone. Obviously most older people are not as bad off as the public generally believes. In fact, people over 64 have a much higher self-image than those in younger age groups, although younger people imagine that self-image declines with age. Perhaps most important is that three out of four older people believe their present life is just as interesting as it ever was.

Of particular interest to geographers are those popular stereotypes of the location, residential situation, and mobility patterns of older people. On the one hand, there is the Sun City image of older people, usually envisioned as a couple moving to a leisure oriented retirement community located in a warm climate. On the other hand, there is an equally strong perception of older people, usually individuals living alone, spending their final years in a nursing home. Neither stereotype, "Sun City" or "God's Waiting Room" is close to accurate. Very few older people migrate from one state to another; in fact relative to other age groups very few older people move. Of those who do, most stay within the same community. Only four to five percent of the elderly reside in institutions—the exact figure depending on the definition of "institution."

As with most stereotypes a more accurate picture emerges when their "yes. . .but" quality is recognized. Yes, poverty is a severe problem for some older people, but only a small percentage report significant difficulties. Yes, health declines with advancing age, but at any one time surprisingly few older people report major life disruptions because of poor health. Yes, some older couples migrate to "Sun City" and some individuals reside in nursing homes, but the vast majority do not. Thus, a more accurate view of old age demands recognizing the diversity that characterizes older people, their life situations and problems. The elderly are not a homogeneous group bound together by the miserable imperatives of old age. There is every reason to believe they are as diverse a group as any cross section of American society and perhaps more so in many ways. Increased leisure time and years of economic independence provide older people with the experience and often opportunities to pursue a wide range of life styles.

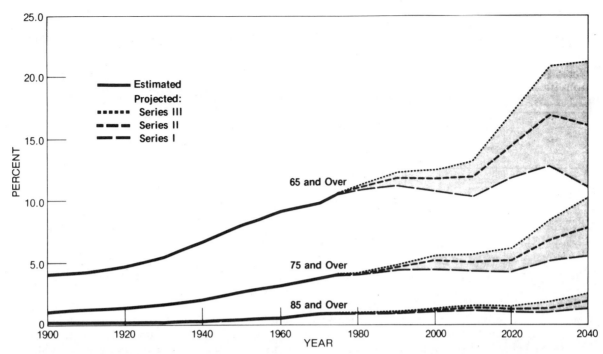

Figure 1. Percent of the total population in the older ages: 1900–2040. Source: U.S. Bureau of the Census, 1976, *Current Population Reports*, *Special Studies*, *Demographic Aspects of Aging and the Older Population in the United States*. Washington, D.C.: U.S. Government Printing Office, Series P–23, No. 59.

The Study of Aging

In studying older people, and especially in searching for theory and accurate generalizations, it is important to recognize the ways older people differ from each other. Such differences may be expressed in a variety of ways such as marital status, racial and cultural heritage, and socioeconomic level. Subgroups of older people identified by these and other characteristics experience old age and its problems differently. For example, an important subgroup is the poor elderly, the majority of whom are also women living alone (Brotman, 1976:11). Although most older people experience health declines, the impact might be much more severe in this group since they may not have anyone to rely upon and cannot purchase the assistance needed to remain residentially independent.

Besides being aware of the diversity among elderly people and the significance of subgroups, it is important to recognize that studies of older people occasionally identify and define the group differently. Many terms have been used to identify the group of people we are concerned with, e.g., aged, elderly, senior citizens, older people, retired people. Contemporary use favors the terms aging and older people. Although these terms lack precision because they could appropriately be applied to many age groups, they have the advantages of being less stigmatic and carry a developmental character. Retired people refers to a group which excludes older people who have not retired and normally includes younger adults who have terminated employment.

The composition of the group being examined is also defined arbitrarily. Most studies use age 60 or 65 as the lower limit for group inclusion. These are commonly used "age breaks" in census data that encompass the early peak retirement years because of Social Security regulations. Selection of one of these ages for inclusion within a study can be important in that many older people remain employed until age 63 or 65. Here, information on the group might be biased towards higher income and other employment related characteristics. There are also more people in the 60 to 65 age cohort than in older cohorts. Thus, the findings of any study of older people must be weighed in terms of span of ages considered.

A frequently employed dichotomy is that of "young-old and old-old" (Neugarten, 1975). Here the period of old age is viewed as encompassing two major phases. The first spans the decade following retirement, that is, ages 65 to 75 and the second is generally considered to be the remainder of the life span. Many researchers have employed this concept, and comparative analyses consistently support the fact that there are significant differences among individuals constituting the two age groups. For example, the young-old are often found to be highly active, in good health, stronger in self-concept, less probably widowed, and more confident in their ability to control their lives. In other words, this group is similar to late middle age except for retirement and its attendant effects. The oldest group consists of those who have most likely experienced the losses and declines of old age. Consequently they are poorer, less healthy, more likely widowed, and in general much less active.

Much of what we presently know about older people is based upon extremely limited information derived from census reports. On a simple basis the

U.S. Government reports selected characteristics of older people, e.g., the number of people by age and sex, the number of retired or employed persons, and household income by age group. Very few of the many items obtained in the census are actually published according to age. Although there is an attempt to increase the amount of information reported on older people in the 1980 Census, there will still be considerably less information available on older people than there will be for other minority groups.

The data problem is even more severe for geographers because very little census information on older people has geographic specificity. Census tract and block data report relatively little information by age, e.g., number of people age 65 and over. Even if we use Public Use Sample records, data gathered on individuals sampled within the census, the geographical information they contain such as the place of residence is limited to specification of a group of counties rather than an address or even a city or county of residence. Because of such limitations, researchers increasingly are forced to acquire primary data from direct interviews with older people. This is a laborious and expensive task if one is to acquire an adequately representative sample. Research is even more difficult because lists of people within a community which specify age of residents seldom exist.

Even when surveys of older people are undertaken, they seldom gather the most appropriate data for the study of aging. By definition such study focuses upon change over time, i.e., how do people or groups change with advancing age? To answer this question we need longitudinal data, data gathered from at least two points in time.

Most aging studies are based upon cross-sectional data, i.e., a comparison of groups defined by different age cohorts surveyed at *one* point of time. Such studies can measure age differences by comparing groups of people at different ages, but cannot describe accurately changes that are attributable solely to the process of aging. These studies usually report group averages that emphasize inter-individual and/or inter-group variation. For example, a study that examines the importance of financial and employment security might reveal significant differences between different age groups. If the older group reported greater concern for security, the researcher would be tempted to conclude that in the course of aging issues related to security become more important. It is quite likely that the older group matured during the period of the Great Depression and therefore its concern with security is more the result of historical event than the aging process. To know definitively that income security becomes more important with advanced age, the groups would have had to have been surveyed at an earlier time. Perhaps there was just as much difference between the two groups many years ago. This inherent difference between age groups is known as cohort effect.

Few studies use longitudinal data because of the obvious costs and time involved, but other problems also arise in longitudinal research designs. One is that samples of people drawn from the same group at different times can vary because of sampling errors. Another is that attrition within the group over time might not be random, e.g., death rates might vary systematically among different subgroups. Finally, it is possible that differences reported by the same group between times one and two could result from period effects, i.e., the extent to which the historical era in which measurements are made affects the results of those measurements.

One of the rarest and most ideal study designs employs panel data. This involves examining the same people at two or more times. Although attrition problems are always present, using panel data has the advantage of revealing change over time in the aging individual and therefore becomes a study of intra-individual (ontogenetic) change. Such data could also be aggregated to determine inter-group change. Even this type of study cannot establish absolutely the changes attributable to aging, cohort, and period effects (Schaie, 1965; Glenn, 1977; and Baltes *et al.*, in press). Most studies of this nature focus on changes with aging while controlling for cohort effects and assume little if any period effect.

We can draw several conclusions from the above. First, readily available data on older people and the process of aging are very limited. Consequently, we know relatively little about older people. Second, only a few studies have examined data that are longitudinal and most desirable for aging research. Thus, there is considerable uncertainty as to what truly characterizes aging in later life and what may result from cohort and period effects. This is especially true of studies comparing elderly cohorts to other age groups. Third, geographic data, even of a cross-sectional nature, are very limited. Therefore, we have sketchy knowledge of the spatial aspects of aging with a few aspects being fairly well developed and others significantly underdeveloped. The aspects presented in this paper are those which have received most attention. Even in these areas, however, numerous questions remain to be answered by future research.

II. THEORETICAL PERSPECTIVES ON AGING

Researchers use theory to explain their findings and to integrate specific knowledge in such a way that they can achieve a clearer understanding of the world than they now possess. The field of social gerontology has developed several widely accepted theories that are relevant to geographical study. It is important that we understand these theories because the theoretical perspective(s) we embrace may strongly influence our interpretation of factual information about older people, their life experiences, and needs. This becomes even more important when conflicting and competing theories exist, as is the case in social gerontology.

This chapter will first present a developmental perspective on aging. A description of some of the relationships between age and level of sensorimotor abilities follows. Then we will consider the major theories of social gerontology from the developmental perspective. The chapter ends by discussing the utility of employing a multidimensional-developmental perspective in studying the spatial aspects of aging.

Developmental Perspective

Aging is a process all organisms experience at all times of life. In our concern with the aged it is too easy to disassociate the latest period of life from that which has gone before. This leads to the treatment of old age as a very different time of life from other times and to a conception of old people as very different from the rest of society. Not only does such an approach impose an unnecessary social stigma on older people, but also obviates one of the most important reasons for studying the elderly, i.e., study of one important stage in life. Most of what we know about society and our use of space implicitly assumes an age-homogeneous society. At best the aged are often viewed as an important minority group. But they are much more than that; they are society at an advanced age. By embracing a developmental view of aging, geographic and other social scientific study of older people can contribute more to general understanding than only the analysis of one more minority group.

The developmental perspective acknowledges that aging is a set of multi-dimensional processes experienced continuously throughout life. Some of the major dimensions are physiological, sociological, and psychological. For example, Figure 2 describes the sociological dimension of aging by the concept of life cycle and the movement from one stage to another over the life span. Here, the typical individual proceeds from the childhood and adolescent stages of the life cycle to a stage of independent living and household formation, family formation, child rearing, empty nest, and retirement. Sociologists have assembled considerable evidence to support this model, although they find substantial variation among individuals, especially during the later portions of the life cycle. A physiological dimension could be added to Figure 2 characterized by stages such as pubescence, the onset of senescence, significant physiological declines perhaps resulting in chronic health problems, the significant decline of certain organs and tissues leading to acute health problems, and ultimately death. The psychological dimension can be described according to any one of a number of psychological attributes, e.g., self concept, intelligence, and feelings of control. Most of the physiological and psychological measures have a common pattern in the typical life span; they generally rise through the first two decades of life reaching maximums and often "plateaus" through the middle years, and decline in the later years.

Obviously the developmental dimensions of life are not orthogonal, i.e., absolutely independent of each other, nor can measures of them be expected to correlate perfectly over the life span among any group or even within any specific individual. We can use these developmental dimensions to identify and characterize the major stages of life and to model in a general way developments leading to the old age stage.

A good example of the developmental perspective and one which is particularly relevant to gerontological study is the dimension of physiological functioning. Medical and biological evidence demonstrate that physiological functioning declines gradually over most of the adult life span often beginning as early as age thirty. As can be seen in Figure 3, these declines are gradual and sympathetic rather than precipitous and occur over the entire adult span, although some functions decline much more rapidly than others. Many compensations are possible to ameliorate the effects of such declines. For most people, then, the basic behavior patterns and ways of life are not dramatically disrupted until the very latest years of life or when one experiences a severe health problem. Within the general trends of physiological change there is a high degree of variation among individuals. Health problems can occur at any age.

Health problems can be defined as either chronic (lasting a long time) or acute (a short-termed problem) with arthritis as a good example of a chronic condition. Most elderly people are coping with some form of chronic illness; approximately 85 percent of the older population report at least one chronic condition. However, only 15 percent find themselves seriously debilitated because of chronic health problems. Although acute health problems affect most people at some point, they often are more serious for older people because of the cumulative impact of the many gradual physiological declines.

This physiological view of aging highlights the problem of defining clearly the stage of old age and characterizing it precisely. In the past, old age was described as a period of senility. Years of research have shown that most symptoms described as senility are manifestations of specific physiological declines, e.g., arteriosclerosis and chronic brain syndrome.

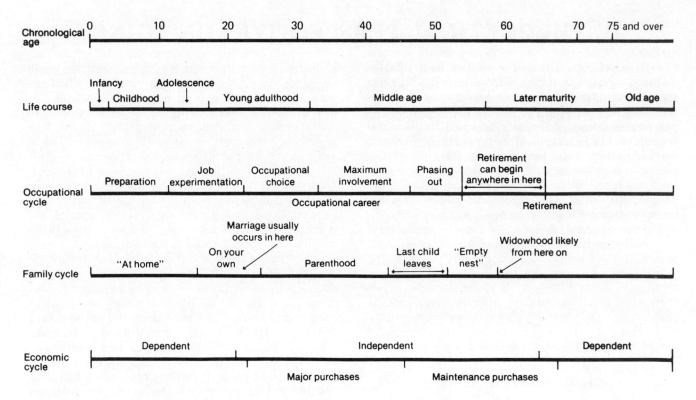

Figure 2. Selected dimensions of life cycle. From Robert C. Atchley, 1975, "The Life Course, Age Grading, and Age-Linked Demands for Decision Making," in Nancy Datan and Leon H. Ginsberg (eds.), *Life-Span Developmental Psychology: Normative Life Crises*. New York: Academic Press, p. 264.

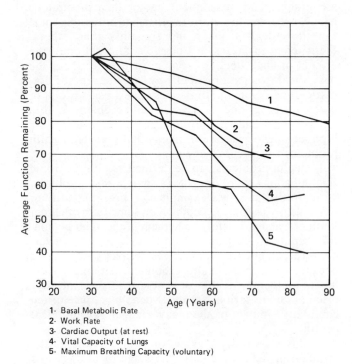

Figure 3. Health declines with increasing age. Redrawn from Nathan W. Shock, 1962, "The Physiology of Aging," *Scientific American*, Vol. 206, pp. 100–110. Used by permission of *Scientific American*.

Although these declines are not reversible they are increasingly ameliorated by medical treatment. Senescence is the commonly accepted term for biological aging. It can be described as a deterioration process in which physiological functions decline, such as those in Figure 3. As a result there is a decline in an organism's general viability and an increase in its vulnerability.

In the later phases of senescence three significant changes can be observed. First, there is a deterioration of critical organs and systems of the body. Often associated with these declines is a heightened vulnerability to disease leading to severe, acute, health problems. A second major change in the physiological process of aging is a notable loss of muscular strength beginning as early as age 40 and associated changes in the nervous system that may result in circulatory problems within the brain. These and related changes often impede one's ability to work and function as well as at an earlier age. It appears that most people adjust to these gradual changing conditions so that behavior and activity patterns are not disrupted noticeably until the very latest stages of life.

The third change and, perhaps most relevant for geographic studies, is the loss of sensory acuity. Most noticeable is the decline in visual acuity, especially in night vision. Farsightedness is common among most people between ages 30 and 35. Although many corrective steps can be taken, several types of visual decline, such as rigidification of the retina, cannot be arrested by medical treatment. Decline in visual acuity can obviously affect spatial movement and behavior. For example, older people who walk very slowly and carefully are generally assumed to have suffered a decline in body strength, balance, and motor control. Visual problems such as an inability to distinguish hazardous cracks in sidewalks or the slope of curb cuts can often be responsible. In addition, there are other sensorimotor declines, such as in hearing ability. Although several effects result from this, the most obvious is a loss of ability to hear in the higher frequency range and, for some, a disturbance in their sense of balance. Again, this can have important implications for studies of spatial movement.

Social Theories of Aging

People also experience declines in other dimensions of life. Pastalan specifies an "Age Loss Continuum" which holds that "as a person continues to age beyond his sixth or seventh decade of life, a number of crucial age-related losses occur and accumulate until ultimately the person will lose all semblances of autonomous being and will depend entirely on others to sustain his very life" (1975:219). Old age, as shown in Table 1, may be viewed as a time when one is likely to lose a spouse, friends, income, and social roles as well as suffer health declines, although the exact age when an individual may experience such losses varies highly. The latest stage of life for most old people is thus seen as a period of cumulative loss and considerable deprivation calling for major personal adjustments.

Following this line of reasoning, one of the earliest social views of aging to develop was disengagement theory (Cumming and Henry, 1961). The theory was designed to be a comprehensive model with universal application and predictive ability. As such it provided a persuasive and coherent framework for much subsequent research (Orbach, 1974). Essentially, disengagement theory defines a process whereby society and the aged individual, in preparation for the individual's impending death and in response to losses in old age, mutually withdraw from each other. The theory is manifest in a declining number of social transactions with advancing age and the permanent loss of many social roles. It presumes that the individual voluntarily withdraws from society and turns increasingly inward. Several gerontologists believe that disengagement accurately reflects what happens to people as they reach very old age, i.e., disengagement describes a real social-physiological stage in the process of aging. Most research questions the voluntary nature of individual withdrawal. This is based on findings that indicate that many older people are happiest when they remain active and engaged. In addition, several recent trends suggest that disengagement is not an inevitable stage in later life. For example, society is more aware of older people and less insistent that they be relegated to a subculture with minority group status. In addition, today older people have better health, economic security, and public visibility. Consequently, they are more active and more vocal in controlling their own futures (Manney, 1975: 18).

Activity theory offers a competitive perspective to disengagement theory. It states that people will try to continue living according to the patterns of their middle years as long as possible, despite the effects of the aging process. There has been far less scholarly treatment of this than disengagement theory, although activity theory is a common guide to action programs for the elderly. It is understandable that many gerontologists would embrace activity theory, since the beginnings of American gerontological study are rooted in the 1930's when strong concerns were articulated about the plight and problems of older persons. Assumptions inherent in activity theory are conveyed by such comments as, "You are remarkable. You never seem to grow old." Statements such as these imply that the older person recognizes the continuing imperatives of the norms of middle age and succeeds in living by them. Unfortunately, the compliment also assumes that it is correct to judge people by the standards of middle age—that an older person should make every effort to remain middle aged. This person would not want to give up habitual roles and activities, as disengagement theory argues, but would strive to continue playing middle-age roles. Research suggests that activity theory applies well to those who are physically healthy and vigorous, which is, of course, an ever larger subgroup of our modern society. But, the theory applies less well to those people in the latest stage of life to whom aging has brought significant physical decline.

A third major social gerontological theory of aging which is just beginning to be examined is continuity theory. The principle assumption of continuity theory is that a person attempts to maintain throughout life familiar and habitual patterns of living; however, a person can be flexible in modifying these patterns to respond to the multiplicity of special combinations of

TABLE 1. THE AGE-LOSS CONTINUUM

Losses	30	40	50	60	70	80	90
Desertion of Children			X				
Loss of Peers				X			
Loss of Spouse				X			
Sensory Output Deterioration					X		
Sensory Acuity Losses				X			
Other Health Problems						X	
Reduced Physical Mobility						X	
Loss of Income				X			
Loss of Roles				X			

Source: Leon A. Pastalan and Daniel H. Carson, 1970. *Spatial Behavior of Older People*. Ann Arbor, Michigan: University of Michigan, Institute of Gerontology. Used by permission.

psychological, biological, and social changes that occur in later life. Thus, although people will want to eat, sleep, work and play as before, they may change the way they go about those activities. They may choose also to replace lost or relinquished roles in the manner by which they adapt to new contingencies. The distinguishing assumption in continuity theory is that a person may adapt in any direction, whereas both activity and disengagement theories propose a unidirectional, normative development in later life. The drawback of continuity theory is that it assumes enormously varied and complex experiential possibilities among the elderly. Because the theory encompasses so much, it is difficult to use as a basis for framing research and for prediction, even though it may best represent what happens to people as they grow old. The appeal of continuity theory is that it attributes to a person a never ending capacity to change. It is an optimistic view of aging. However, a theory's appeal is no measure of its worth, and the validity and utility of continuity theory are largely unknown.

In summary, it is clear that the field of social gerontology requires more theoretical development and that no current theory presently commands the allegiance of all or even most of the people working in the field. As Atchley (1972: 39) observes:

> ...none of the existing theories can completely explain aging in modern society. The responsible investigator must constantly compare the situation he is attempting to explain with the existing theories and be ready to invent a new explanation if none of the ready-made ones works.

Employing the Multidimensional-Developmental Perspective

The theoretical perspective one employs strongly influences interpretation of study results. For example, an investigation of the spatial behavior of older persons might compare activity patterns of older people with those of younger adults. Some studies have already found that the spatial behavior of older people is significantly less in this comparison (Marble, Hanson, and Hanson, 1973). If one subscribes to disengagement theory, the explanation for such findings would be that the older person manifests disengagement in more limited spatial behavior. More important would be the reseacher's positing a possible prescription: That because older people are basically seeking disengagement, society should plan physical environments and service delivery programs to enhance that effort. On the other hand, if one subscribes to activity theory, the same empirical findings, i.e., more limited spatial behavior by older people, might result in recommendations for programs that attempt to enhance the activity opportunities available to the older person.

In lieu of a simple widely accepted theory of aging, the multidimensional-developmental perspective can be employed to explain much of what is known about old age. For example, we can resolve some of the obvious conflicts between disengagement and activity theories by placing them in a multidimensional-

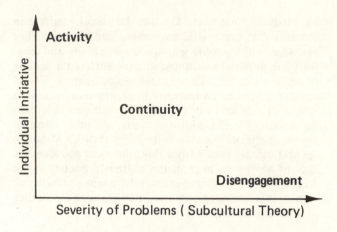

Figure 4. Major theories of social gerontology.

developmental context where they might be viewed as coping strategies. Figure 4 presents such a view and it is developed further in Berghorn *et al.*, *The Urban Elderly*, 1978. Older people with very severe problems, perhaps those having suffered significant health declines or other losses, might employ a disengagement strategy in coping with life. Others, whose problems are less severe and who have greater personal and other resources, can exercise more individual initiative and employ an activity strategy well into the later years of life. Between these extremes continuity theory predicts modification of earlier activity patterns and suggests that many strategies can be employed in the transition from a very active older life to one of considerable disengagement. Thus, the developmental view of the aging process helps resolve some theoretical conflicts. It also provides explanation for contradictory research findings by questioning the relevance of the variable "age" itself. That is, individuals who are 85 might be much "younger" in terms of their positions on any one or all life dimensions.

It is important to keep this perspective in mind when examining spatial aspects of aging in that it indicates the many ways old age differs from other stages in life. Awareness of the declines and losses that attend old age for many people helps us understand the problems older people share and suggests ways in which special programs can be designed to improve their quality of life. Such awareness also explains why older persons are more sensitive to environmental influences and how environments can be redesigned to enhance their life experiences. However, this perspective also cautions us against viewing old age and old people as being an entirely unique time of life or a totally distinct group. Needs, desires, and activity patterns may change in old age, but there is considerable continuity with other stages of life. Experience gained throughout the course of life is not forgotten but represents an enriched personal resource for individuals to draw upon in old age.

Finally, this perspective calls attention to the wide range of diversity among older people. Although age is the criterion variable that distinguishes this group from the remainder of society, it is clear that all older people do not share the same set of old age experiences, declines, and losses. Study of aging often demands that the study group be disaggregated to meaningful subgroups. For example, a study of elderly migration might conclude that many old people relocate after years of residing in the same place because of health declines and other losses leading to a severe reduction in the ability to take care of themselves. However, many elderly migrants have not experienced these changes and consequently must be moving for different reasons. Some may relocate to enhance their level of activity, perhaps moving to a retirement community. Similarly, when we study the issue of age concentration, it is important to realize that some older people might prefer age homogeneous social settings and living arrangements whereas others do not.

In summary, then, the multidimensional-developmental perspective reveals that aging is a gradual process of change experienced throughout life. Old age is one important stage of life—a stage when many people suffer predictable health declines and a variety of losses. However, it is as difficult to identify precisely when old age begins as it is to characterize it precisely. This is because of the vast interindividual variability that also makes it imperative for researchers to classify the elderly population into meaningful subgroups.

It is important that we keep in mind this perspective and these points as we consider the spatial aspects of aging presented in the next few chapters. This will facilitate a critique of existing knowledge and help us explain study findings without becoming overly involved in theoretical controversy.

III. SPATIAL PATTERNS OF OLDER AMERICANS

Demographers often refer to the U.S. as an "aging population" (Cowgill, 1970: 27), because the elderly segment of our society is constantly increasing, and forecasts into the future indicate elderly citizens occupying even greater proportions of our population than is the case today. This chapter begins with an examination of the historical pattern of elderly population and a discussion of the processes which have produced this growth. Next, we consider the geographical distribution of the elderly population as it has evolved over time and we will examine patterns of elderly concentration at several spatial scales ranging from national to local levels. Finally we will give attention to the processes by which patterns of concentration change over time.

Growth of the Elderly Population

The tremendous growth in the number of older people within the U.S. is clearly demonstrated in Census statistics in Table 2. In 1900, there were only 3.1 million people aged 65 and over, comprising 4.1 percent of the population. Thirty years later, there were 6.7 million, or 5.4 percent of the population. Over the next 30 years, these numbers had jumped to 16.7 million people or by 9.2 percent. In 1975, 22.4 million or 10.5 percent of the population were classified as elderly. Thus, in the span of one lifetime, approximately 75 years, the elderly population of the U.S. increased over seven-fold and the proportion of elderly citizens increased by a factor of more than two. Estimates for the year 2000 indicate that the percent of total U.S. population age 65 and over will increase only slightly to approximately 12 percent. However, the absolute number of older Americans will be nearly half again as large as it is today. Although the proportion of aged in our society is slowly increasing, the total numbers of older people are growing at an increasingly rapid rate.

TABLE 2. U.S. POPULATION AGE 65 AND OVER, 1900–2000

Year	No. (Millions)	% Total Population
1900	3.1	4.1
1910	4.0	4.3
1920	5.0	4.6
1930	6.7	5.4
1940	9.0	6.8
1950	12.4	8.1
1960	16.7	9.2
1970	20.1	9.8
1975	22.4	10.5
Projections:		
1980	24.5	11.0
1990	29.0	11.7
2000	31.0	11.7

Source: United States Bureau of the Census, 1976:9.

These trends reflect changes in fertility, mortality, and immigration (Coale, 1964). The first, fertility, has been the most significant factor in influencing both the numbers and the proportion of aged people in the population. Continually rising birth rates that were characteristic of this country until about 1920 were responsible for the rapid increase in numbers of people reaching age 65 today. After 1920, however, the birth rate began to decline and for this reason we see increasing proportions of older people in the society. There are fewer young people relative to the number of elderly individuals. This trend was interrupted by the post World War II Baby Boom which will have a dramatic impact on the size of the elderly population beginning in the second decade of the next century. Since the 1960's, however, there has been a sharp decline in the birth rate, and consequently, the rate of growth of the aging group should also begin to decline between 2020 and 2030.

These fluctuations and trends are depicted in the population pyramids in Figure 5. In 1900, the pyramid has a symmetry which reflects a population normally distributed through age cohorts, that is, there are more people of younger ages relative to any cohort. The pyramid for 1940 reflects declining birth rates in the younger age cohorts, 0–4 and 5–9, which constitute a smaller proportion of the entire population than might be expected. This "indentation" in the pyramid is carried up to older cohorts, ages 30 to 40, as the population ages 30 years to the 1970 pyramid. In 1970, the post-war Baby Boom is clearly visible in lower cohorts and the declining birth rate is reflected at the youngest age groups. It is relatively easy to forecast the gross shape of the pyramid into the future, perhaps 40 years from now when the large cohorts ages 10 through 20 in 1970 constitute the aged population in the years 2030 through 2040. If current low birth rates continue and zero population growth characterizes our society, it is clear that the proportion of older persons within the U.S. in the future will increase dramatically. It is likely that in our lifetime we shall see older persons constituting as much as 20 percent or more of the U.S. population.

As one would expect, the mortality rate has also been declining since 1900. This decline is most evident at the lower end of the age pyramid. Problems of childbearing and delivery, childhood diseases, and mortality relating to diet and sanitation have all been brought under control. The consequence of these improvements is usually referred to as increased life expectancy. In 1900, the average life expectancy of an individual was 49 years; by 1973 this had increased to 71.5 years. As Table 3 shows, the age at which average remaining lifetime equals ten years has increased by only five years since 1900. In other words, an individual who survived birth and childhood in the early part of the century had nearly the same chances of living into old age as an individual born today. The modest improvements in mortality rates of older persons are primarily a result of our inability to control the major causes of death (heart disease, cancer, and stroke) within this group (Coale, 1964). Thus, the major impact of reduced mortality rates arises from the larger number of people who live to old age. Present medical research into the primary causes of death might make this a more significant factor in the future.

The third major factor contributing to demographic composition is immigration. Generally, immigrants tend to be younger people and thus the initial effect is to reduce the proportion of older persons in the population. Because of the significant immigration prior to World War I this process has contributed significantly to the large numbers of elderly appearing in the population within recent decades. Immigrants have added to a particular birth cohort, a group of people born in the same period, and moves with it through time. Because immigration declined after World War I, it is

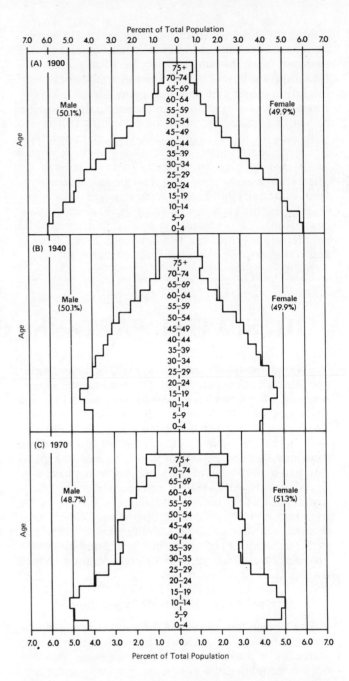

Figure 5. Age-sex population pyramids for the United States. Redrawn by permission from Neal E. Cutler and Robert A. Harootyan, 1975, "Demography of the Aged," in Diana S. Woodruff and James E. Birren (eds.), *Aging: Scientific Perspectives and Social Issues*. New York: D. Van Nostrand Co., p. 36. © 1975 by Litton Educational Publishing, Inc.

expected to play a lesser role in expanding the future elderly population.

In summary, then, birth rates, death rates, and, at various periods, immigration are the primary controls of the present and future distribution of the elderly population. When these factors are fairly stable one

TABLE 3. INCREASES IN AVERAGE
LIFE SPAN REMAINING

Year	Age at Which Average Remaining Lifetime Equals 10.0 Years
1900	68.6
1930	69.1
1960	72.5
1970	73.7

Source: United States Bureau of the Census, 1976a:11.

can forecast future populations of older persons at some future date. When this is done we see that the U.S. is indeed an aging society and that the elderly will be even more important in the future.

National Pattern of Concentration

For geographers and many others concerned with the older segment of society, it is just as important to know where older people are located as it is to know that the United States has an aging population. When we examine the spatial distribution of older persons, considerable systematic variation becomes apparent and distinct spatial patterns appear. On close analysis, the geographical patterns of older people appear to be highly dynamic.

In general, the distribution of older persons corresponds closely to that of the total population, shown in Table 4. The largest states have the largest number of aged persons. In fact, only 10 states account for 54 percent of all older persons in this country. This distribution has not changed markedly over time. There is considerable variation in the concentration of elderly within state populations ranging from as much as 16 percent in Florida to as little as two percent in Alaska. This concentration has changed a great deal over time and has produced a distinctive regional pattern of elderly concentration.

Changes in state concentrations of older persons since 1910 are shown in Table 5 and Figure 6. The increasing proportion of elderly within the U.S. can be seen in the progressive "darkening" of the map over time. The increase is not uniformly distributed among the states and the variation in the proportion of older persons within state populations has increased dramatically. In 1910, only northern New England had a considerable concentration of elderly persons whereas the rest of the country reported fairly uniform and very low percentages of older persons. Since 1910 some states, particularly those in the west and southeast, consistently report low concentrations that fall below the national average. Other states show large increases and have concentrations of older people far in excess of the national average. Today, there is marked contrast among regions with the most notable concentrations in the central states, the northeast, and Florida.

During this period, several states recorded surprisingly large increases. For example, Florida in 1950 had 8.5 percent of its population classified as elderly compared to 1970 when it had 14.5 percent. During this 20-year period, Florida rose from 21st position to first when the states are ranked according to the proportion of elderly in the population. Similarly, Arkansas rose from 29th position in 1950 (7.8 percent) to second (12.3 percent) in 1970. More recent data in Table 4 reveal that the pattern of regional contrasts is intensifying. Florida still leads the nation with 16.4 percent elderly and Arkansas is still second with 13.1 percent. Although minor changes took place in the rankings, they reinforce the general pattern of change since early in the present century.

A recent study of the U.S. examines changing concentrations of elderly within county populations (Graff and Wiseman, 1978). In general the pattern of county concentration also supports the regional pattern shown in Figure 6. As might be expected when we consider smaller spatial units, the range of concentration increases, with a 1970 low of 0.4 percent in Chattahoochee County, Georgia, and a high of 35 percent in Charlotte County, Florida. More importantly, this study reveals that within many states the concentration of elderly is not uniformly distributed. Elderly concentrations are much higher in rural and central city counties. This is reflected in Figure 7 which displays those counties whose elderly concentration increased by more than twice the national average increase over the period 1950 to 1970. Non-metropolitan counties, particularly in the Great Plains, Gulf Coastal Plains, and the Appalachian region have experienced large recent increases. Counties noted for vacation and recreational amenities, e.g., in Florida, the Ozarks, northern Michigan, Wisconsin, and Minnesota, as well as counties scattered throughout the west and southwest, also report growth in their elderly populations. Finally, counties containing central cities of large Standard Metropolitan Statistical Areas (SMSAs) reveal increased concentrations. Thus, within states whose concentration of elderly is increasing, the counties most responsible for that growth are characterized as being rural, recreational, or central metropolitan.

Urban Concentrations

In 1975 nearly 71 percent of all older Americans resided in metropolitan areas. This is similar to the non-elderly population, 74 percent of whom were classified as urban. A popular view of the location of elderly within urban areas is that most reside in "elderly ghettos." Although this concept is not well defined, it is often equated with high concentrations of older people.

There is, however, considerable controversy about whether or not elderly ghettos exist. As early as 1962, Hoover and Vernon identified a large concentration of older people in Manhattan. Others, such as Palmore and Whittington (1971) noted that the elderly

TABLE 4. U.S. POPULATION AGE 65 AND OVER, 1976

State	Total	Age 65+	Elderly as Percent of State Population	Elderly as Percent of U.S. Elderly Population
California	21,519,700	2,120,700	9.9	9.04
New York	18,083,700	2,067,600	11.4	8.81
Pennsylvania	11,862,100	1,404,100	11.8	5.98
Florida	8,420,800	1,383,300	16.4	5.89
Texas	12,487,700	1,193,000	9.6	5.08
Illinois	11,229,200	1,171,000	10.4	4.99
Ohio	10,689,800	1,088,800	10.2	4.64
Michigan	9,104,100	833,600	9.2	3.55
New Jersey	7,336,300	786,700	10.7	3.35
Massachusetts	5,809,100	681,700	11.7	2.90
Missouri	4,788,500	608,200	12.7	2.59
North Carolina	5,469,000	572,800	9.4	2.44
Indiana	5,301,600	540,400	10.2	2.30
Wisconsin	4,608,800	522,600	11.3	2.23
Delaware	582,100	51,400	8.8	2.19
Minnesota	3,964,700	455,400	11.2	1.94
Tennessee	4,214,300	452,800	10.7	1.93
Georgia	4,970,200	443,400	8.9	1.89
Virginia	5,032,300	440,500	8.8	1.88
Alabama	3,664,900	388,200	10.6	1.65
Washington	3,611,800	373,500	10.3	1.59
Kentucky	3,427,900	372,700	10.9	1.59
Iowa	2,869,800	366,700	12.8	1.56
Louisiana	3,841,000	354,600	9.2	1.51
Maryland	4,144,500	349,900	8.4	1.49
Oklahoma	2,766,400	339,500	12.3	1.45
Connecticut	3,117,100	330,400	10.6	1.41
Kansas	2,310,000	288,600	12.5	1.23
Arkansas	2,109,300	277,400	13.2	1.18
Oregon	2,328,700	266,100	11.4	1.13
Mississippi	2,354,400	259,300	11.0	1.10
South Carolina	2,848,300	239,800	8.4	1.02
Arizona	2,770,400	235,200	10.4	1.00
Colorado	2,582,100	217,700	8.4	0.93
West Virginia	1,820,700	214,400	11.8	0.91
Nebraska	1,552,900	195,700	12.6	0.83
Maine	1,069,900	127,700	11.9	0.54
Rhode Island	926,600	115,800	12.5	0.49
Utah	1,228,000	94,300	7.7	0.40
New Mexico	1,168,100	94,000	8.0	0.40
New Hampshire	822,300	91,000	11.1	0.39
South Dakota	686,000	86,400	12.6	0.37
Idaho	830,600	81,400	9.8	0.35
Montana	752,700	76,500	10.2	0.33
North Dakota	643,300	74,500	11.6	0.32
District of Columbia	701,800	72,400	10.3	0.31
Hawaii	886,600	59,800	6.7	0.25
Vermont	476,300	53,300	11.2	0.23
Nevada	609,900	46,700	7.7	0.20
Wyoming	390,400	34,300	8.8	0.15
Alaska	382,000	9,000	2.4	0.04

Source: U.S. Department of Health, Education, and Welfare, 1976.

TABLE 5. PERCENT OF U.S. POPULATION AGE 65 AND OVER, 1910-1970

State	1910	1930	1950	1970
Alabama	3.04	3.74	6.50	9.47
Alaska	1.56	5.08	3.88	2.33
Arizona	2.94	3.67	5.87	9.09
Arkansas	2.86	4.10	7.85	12.38
California	5.26	6.45	8.45	9.03
Colorado	3.38	5.98	8.75	8.52
Connecticut	5.38	5.79	8.82	9.53
Delaware	4.95	7.14	8.18	8.03
District of Columbia	5.14	5.54	7.11	9.38
Florida	2.92	4.84	8.55	14.57
Georgia	3.10	3.88	6.39	8.00
Hawaii	1.56	2.17	4.00	5.72
Idaho	2.76	4.94	7.47	9.54
Illinois	4.31	5.52	8.65	9.84
Indiana	5.52	7.19	9.18	9.51
Iowa	5.62	7.45	10.42	12.39
Kansas	5.20	6.86	10.18	11.84
Kentucky	4.10	5.43	7.98	10.47
Louisiana	3.02	3.62	6.59	8.43
Maine	8.22	8.66	10.28	11.59
Maryland	4.71	5.70	7.00	7.65
Massachusetts	5.20	6.45	9.98	11.18
Michigan	5.59	5.27	7.25	8.48
Minnesota	4.14	6.36	9.02	10.75
Mississippi	3.01	3.83	7.02	10.01
Missouri	4.56	6.75	10.29	11.99
Montana	2.39	5.02	8.63	9.94
Nebraska	4.28	6.24	9.80	12.41
Nevada	3.66	5.49	6.88	6.34
New Hampshire	7.89	9.03	10.88	10.57
New Jersey	4.22	4.97	8.15	9.72
New Mexico	3.06	4.02	4.85	6.99
New York	4.59	5.30	8.48	10.75
North Carolina	3.54	3.66	5.54	8.15
North Dakota	2.25	4.41	7.74	10.68
Ohio	5.50	6.24	8.92	9.37
Oklahoma	2.47	4.05	8.69	11.72
Oregon	4.16	7.02	8.74	10.86
Pennsylvania	4.25	5.27	8.45	10.79
Rhode Island	4.60	5.82	8.84	10.98
South Carolina	2.90	3.28	5.43	7.37
South Dakota	3.25	5.34	8.42	12.01
Tennessee	3.80	4.55	7.14	9.79
Texas	2.85	3.98	6.65	8.86
Utah	3.22	4.53	6.10	7.37
Vermont	8.15	8.61	10.58	10.59
Virginia	4.12	4.83	6.48	7.81
Washington	3.24	6.53	8.87	9.45
West Virginia	3.44	4.22	6.93	11.12
Wisconsin	5.10	6.53	9.02	10.71
Wyoming	2.05	3.98	6.19	9.04

Source: United States Bureau of the Census, 1976b.

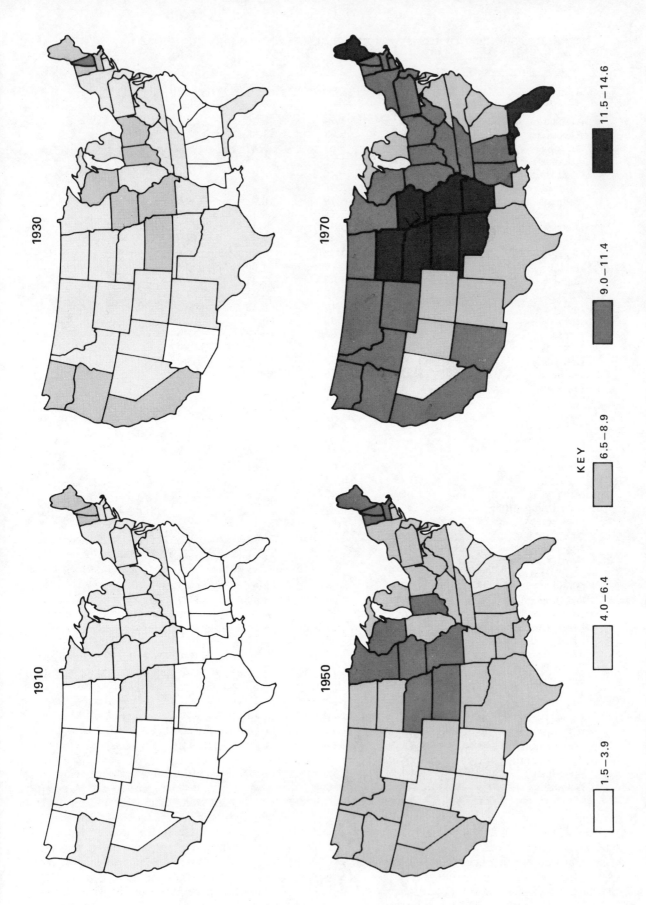

Figure 6. Percent of state population age 65 and over, 1910–1970. Calculated from U.S. Bureau of the Census, 1976, *Current Population Reports, Special Studies, Demographic Aspects of Aging and the Older Population in the United States*. Washington, D.C.: U.S. Government Printing Office, Series P–23, No. 59.

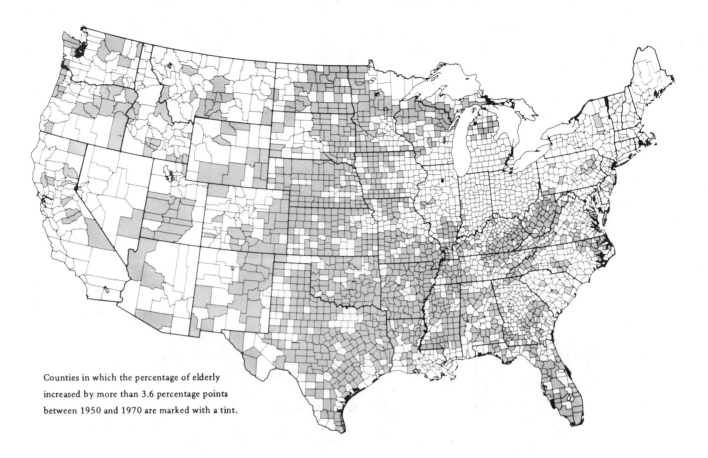

Counties in which the percentage of elderly increased by more than 3.6 percentage points between 1950 and 1970 are marked with a tint.

Figure 7. Counties experiencing a large increase in percentage of elderly people, 1950–1970. From Thomas O. Graff and Robert F. Wiseman, 1978, "Changing Concentrations of Older Americans," *The Geographical Review*, Vol. 68, No. 4, Fig. 3. Used by permission of the American Geographical Society.

tended to be concentrated in rural and central city locations and were underrepresented in suburban locations. In 1971 Johnston described a "senile CBD" in Wellington, New Zealand. Similarly, Cowgill and Ostertag (1962) demonstrated the concentration of older people in the city of Wichita as shown in Figure 8. They concluded that a considerable concentration of aged persons existed near the city's center and that this pattern appeared to persist throught time. Birdsall and Gunville (1977) also demonstrated the existence of intraurban concentrations of older persons in a spatial analysis of age, sex, and race at the census tract level in Washington, D.C. over a 30-year period. A recent study of ten SMSAs concluded that elderly concentrations are more pronounced in newer, growing cities and less apparent in older, declining urban areas (Kennedy and DeJong, 1977). All of these studies affirm the existence of elderly ghettos.

On the other hand, Hiltner and Smith (1974a, 1974b) found that the elderly are not concentrated disproportionately within a single area or even a few neighborhoods. In a series of studies that examined an index of concentration of older people in neighborhoods relative to the entire elderly population, they concluded that the elderly are not concentrated heavily within only a few neighborhoods (Smith and Hiltner, 1975). Furthermore their examination of a 30-year period for Toledo, Ohio indicated no significant increase in the intraurban concentration of older people. They found that the elderly were substantially less concentrated than blacks, a group whose spatial concentration in urban areas has long been recognized. In fact, the index of concentration for the elderly seldom reached 25 percent of its value for blacks. In a similar study of Cleveland and San Diego, undertaken at the census block level, Pampel and Choldin (1978) reported some concentrations of older people occurring within inner city neighborhoods near the CBD, but over the entire city and the entire elderly population, they found older people were more dispersed than concentrated. Many of these studies also examined neighborhood and housing characteristics thought to characterize concentrations of older people. They report that some neighborhoods with a high concentration of elderly have a prevalence of multi-unit housing structures, low housing values, and are located near the CBD. They conclude that the bulk of the urban elderly do not reside in these aged ghettos.

At first glance the literature cited above appears to be contradictory; some studies document the existence of urban elderly ghettos and other studies demonstrate that older persons are not highly concentrated within the urban environment. To a large extent this results from the lack of a clear definition of the

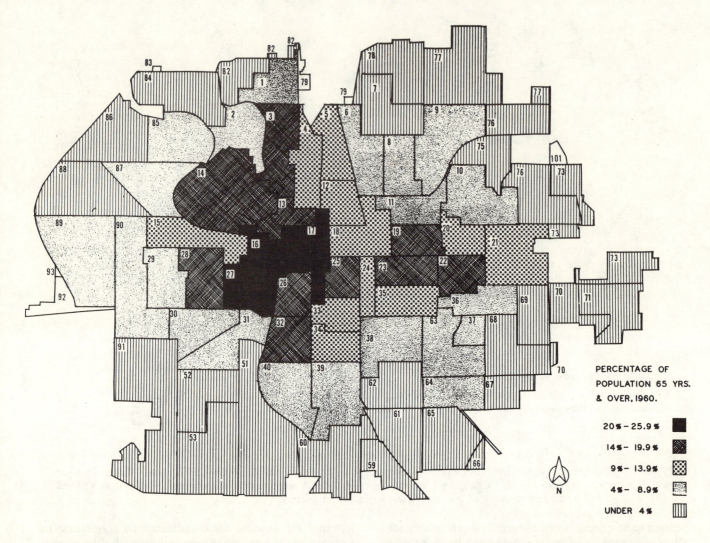

Figure 8. Distribution of elderly in Wichita, Kansas. From Donald O. Cowgill and F. Samuel Ostertag, Jr., 1962, *The People of Wichita, 1960*. Wichita, Kans.: Urban Studies Center, p. 22. Used by permission of The Urban Studies Center, Wichita State University.

terms ghetto and concentration. In addition, the issue is complicated by the variety of research methods that have been employed in these studies. For example, different research findings would result from studies that examined a central city or an entire SMSA. In an SMSA study, one would expect to see central city concentrations of older persons strongly contrasted with the very light densities of older persons found in suburban areas. On the other hand, studies confined to a central city or to the inner city, might find aged concentrations to be much less noticeable or even nonexistent because entire central city counties have high concentrations of elderly (as in Figure 7). Another complication arises from the different spatial units of analysis employed in these studies. It would not be difficult to find high concentrations of older persons measured within census block populations, whereas it would be more difficult to find similarly high concentrations of elderly within much larger census tract populations. Furthermore, some studies use the entire city's elderly population as the basis for producing a measure of concentration whereas others calculate concentration on the basis of total population.

Given these problems what can we conclude about the distribution of older persons within urban areas? It is clear that the majority of elderly are not heavily concentrated in a few urban neighborhoods. Furthermore it appears doubtful that the elderly are tending towards greater concentration. There undoubtedly exist neighborhoods at either the census block or census tract levels that have very high concentrations of older persons, occasionally in excess of 30 percent of the total tract or block population. These neighborhoods characteristically are found in older portions of the city, having older housing stock and high proportions of multiple family dwelling units. In some cases these are neighborhoods in transition. It must be remembered that the majority of urban elderly generally do not reside in such settings. The most general statement one can make about the urban distribution of older persons is that they show high concentrations in older neighborhoods near the

CBD, and that this distribution progressively declines as one moves outward towards suburban portions of the urban area where very few elderly people reside today.

Processes Producing Elderly Concentrations

The locational patterns identified above are the result of several processes, many of which operate simultaneously. The most fundamental process is that of "aging-in-place." This is defined as the movement of a younger cohort to an elderly one simply as a result of the passage of time. Because older cohorts of the population have relatively low migration rates, elderly concentrations can be forecast into the future largely on the basis of aging-in-place. Other processes often work in concert with aging-in-place to further accelerate the development of elderly concentrations. Many rural counties and even states report disproportionately large concentrations that would not exist if younger cohorts had not out-migrated from these locations during earlier periods. Most migration is age-specific and demographers have repeatedly shown that it is the younger adult-age cohorts that most often migrate long distances from their home communities (Roseman, 1977). The past several decades have witnessed massive rural-to-urban migrations, and through the decade of the sixties massive south-to-north migrations as well. When a community loses a large proportion of its younger adults the relative concentration of older persons increases. Much of the explanation for concentration patterns shown in Figure 6 and 7 is attributable to the processes of aging-in-place combined with out-migration of younger cohorts.

To the extent that elderly ghettos exist and large inner city portions of urban areas display disproportionately high concentrations of older persons, the same processes that produce concentrations at other spatial scales are important here. The suburbanization of younger adult cohorts in major metropolitan centers results in an older, aging-in-place population that is disproportionately concentrated in central cities and can be noted in Figure 7 by the increased concentration of older persons in the central city counties of major SMSAs such as New York City and Detroit.

We must not forget that the out-migration of younger groups is accompanied by their in-migration elsewhere. Thus, regions, states, counties, and portions of the urban environment receiving large numbers of younger people generally record low proportions of elderly. States and counties, whose economies are expanding such that employment opportunities and wages are increasing, attract younger migrants in such large numbers that even a large number of elderly people becomes proportionately small. This is the case in California, Arizona, and Colorado. Although the motivation of younger cohort in-migration to suburban communities is different, the effect is similar—low concentrations of older people.

A third major process affecting concentrations of elderly persons is that of elderly migration. Traditionally this has been a minor process, but over the past several decades it has become more important. Because of the spatial nature of elderly migration, discussed in considerable detail in the next chapter, only a few states are being dramatically affected by it. Obviously elderly in-migration is primarily responsible for the increased concentrations of older persons reported in such states as Florida, Arkansas, and Missouri.

For several reasons the process of elderly migration is expected to become more influential in determining future concentrations of older persons. In the past, migration upon retirement was a phenomenon limited primarily to the wealthiest Americans. Recently the financial circumstances of older Americans has improved dramatically (Population Reference Bureau, 1975). General economic advances have provided rising incomes, increases in home ownership, and improved pension benefits. In addition, the recent, dramatic inflation in property values has resulted in a "paper profit" of substantial proportions so that the sale of one's home can provide much of the capital needed for retirement migration to a more desirable location. Moreover, the general rise in mobility, particularly expanded vacation travel, has produced a greater awareness of and familiarity with potential retirement communities. These and other factors, such as friends and acquaintances who have successfully moved to retirement communities, will reinforce concentrations of older persons in traditional retirement states such as Florida.

In summary, the locational distribution of older people is highly variable at all spatial scales. Undeniably there exist regions, states, county groups, and urban neighborhoods that have disproportionately large concentrations of elderly people. Patterns of concentration, particularly at regional, state, and county levels are highly dynamic. Aging-in-place and relatively low migration rates for older people explain much of the variations in these patterns and should facilitate locational forecasts of future elderly concentrations. However, migration of younger groups which affects elderly concentration is more difficult to forecast. The massive rural-to-urban and south-to-north migration patterns of recent decades are now reversing. In addition, migration of older people themselves is growing and because of its unique spatial patterns, considered in the next chapter, will become more important in affecting the distribution of older Americans.

IV. ELDERLY MIGRATION

Traditionally, demographers, geographers, and others have concentrated their migration research on labor force movement whereas aged migration has received relatively little attention. In addition, the few studies that do exist are predicated upon the assumption that elderly migration is only slightly different from general population movements. We are now learning that elderly migrants, particularly those who move long distances, are very different from younger migrants in terms of socio-economic characteristics, the motivations for migration, and the spatial pattern of that migration. Some studies even suggest that elderly migration is a leading indicator of changing trends observed in general population migration patterns and as such warrants considerably more detailed investigation than it has received (Roseman, 1977: 29).

This chapter presents what is currently known about elderly migration. It begins with an examination of mobility rates for older persons compared to other age cohorts. Next, it will present patterns of elderly migration at both the national and local scales. Finally, as is the case in the preceding chapter, we will devote considerable attention to the processes which are thought to produce these patterns.

Mobility Rates

As shown in Figure 9 mobility rates for the United States population vary widely across the life span. Rossi (1955) and many others have demonstrated that the majority of individual moves are associated with change from one life stage to another. Superimposed on the mobility rate graph are various dimensions of what might be termed a general life cycle. Other life dimensions such as the physiological and psychological might be added. In this generalized depiction of the various stages in life development, it can be seen that certain characteristics are associated with high and low mobility rates. For example, the period of life having the highest mobility rate is characterized by the transition from adolescence to young adulthood, a period of job experimentation and occupational choice, household formation and family formation, and in general, the transition from dependent to independent economic status. It is thought that reaching critical points on these dimensions in the life cycle produces changes in housing needs and preferences and stimulates a strong consideration of a decision to move (Rossi, 1955; Leslie and Richardson, 1961; and Yee and Van Arsdol, 1977). Thus, when abrupt changes occur in family structure or on other dimensions of the life cycle there is a higher likelihood of residential change. So, upon graduation, career initiation, marriage, family expansion, promotion, and retirement, the probabilities of moving are high.

Over the life span, then, there is considerable variation in the probability of residential change. (See Figure 9.) The earliest period of high mobility probability, ages 0 to 18, is one in which the individual has little control or influence in the decision making process. Departure from the parental home and initiation of a separate household leads to significant changes in living arrangements and an increase in mobility rates. After the period of family formation, mobility rates continuously decline and reach life-time lows through the pre-retirement period. There is a modest increase in mobility rates during the years of peak retirement activity followed by very low mobility until the latest stage of life has been reached. Then there is a modest rise in residential change. Clearly, mobility rates of the elderly are very low relative to other age cohorts, indicating strong reluctance on the part of older people to move.

Despite low rates of mobility among elderly cohorts, there are considerable numbers of older people involved in residential relocation (local move) and migration (long distance move). Between 1965 and 1970, 28 percent of the population aged 65 and older moved at least once: 18 percent relocated within the same county, 4.5 percent moved elsewhere within the state, 3.8 percent migrated to different states, and 1.7 percent moved to other countries. Although elderly mobility rates have been fairly stable over the past 25 years, the growing number of older persons results in even larger numbers of elderly persons changing residence.

Researchers examining mobility rate data for just the later years of life believe that the retirement "bulge" as shown in Figure 10 is associated with the desire to obtain residential as well as recreational amenities, whereas later moves reflect the need for obtaining medical or living assistance (Golant, 1977; Wiseman and Roseman, 1979). If mobility rates are disaggregated into a dichotomy which distinguishes between local movers or those who relocate within the same county, and long-distance migrants, there are nearly twice as many local moves. Most of the retirement movement may be attributed to long distance migrants who tend to be younger elderly couples relocating to areas possessing many residential and recreational amenities. During the retirement period the probability of a local move gradually declines but increases during the last years when widowhood and the need for medical and personal assistance result in the loss of residential independence for many elderly.

National Patterns of Elderly Migration

Studies of elderly migration at the national scale often analyze census data, particularly state rates of in, out, and net migration. Generally researchers use net migration, the difference between in and out, in these studies. A recent study by Barsby and Cox (1975) typifies this approach. State net migration rates are correlated with independent variables describing various population characteristics such as past migration rate, welfare and tax levels, income and education

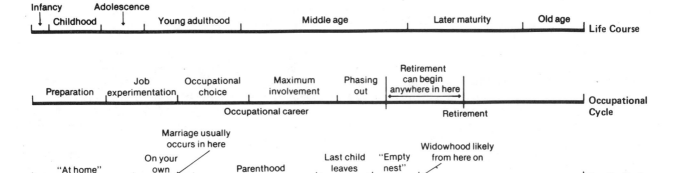
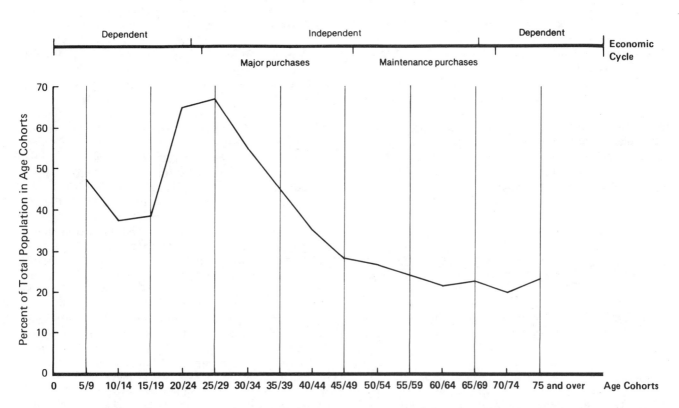

Figure 9. Mobility rates over the life span. Rates calculated from U.S. Bureau of the Census, 1973, *Census of Population: 1970, Subject Reports, Mobility for States and the Nation*. Washington, D.C.: U.S. Government Printing Office, Final Report PC (2)–2B. Life Span redrawn from Robert C. Atchley, 1975, "The Life Course, Age Grading, and Age-Linked Demands for Decision Making," by permission of the author in Nancy Datan and Leon H. Ginsberg (eds.), *Life-Span Developmental Psychology: Normative Life Crises*. © New York: Academic Press, p. 264.

levels, labor force status, and tenure status. The study places emphasis on economic variables thought to be key determinants of migration. The study concludes that past migration experience, high income and educational level, low labor force participation rates, and high job turnover are positively related to migration rates for older persons. In general, this study finds relatively weak associations and poor statistical explanation of elderly migration rates.

This is not surprising since most elderly migrants are outside of the labor force. A recent study (Cebula, 1974) reveals that economic variables are not closely associated with elderly migration. Rather he finds that temperature differentials, the availability of recreational facilities, and medical care are most important. This and other studies conclude that environment, interpersonal relations, health, and a search for residential amenities are probably the most influential factors in an older person's decision to move (Goldstein, 1967; Walker and Price, 1975; Svart, 1976; and Chevan and Fischer, 1978). Clearly, migration motivations for older people are different from those of most younger groups.

Elderly migration differs from younger population migration in other ways as well. For example, in return migration older people are more likely to return to their states of birth (Serow, 1978). Distance has less effect on elderly migration as Catau's (1978) study

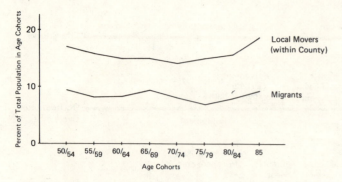

Figure 10. Mobility rates for select cohorts of U.S. population, 1975–1976. Calculated from U.S. Bureau of the Census, 1973, *Census of Population: 1970, Characteristics of the Population*, Part I. Washington, D.C.: U.S. Government Printing Office.

of 230 elderly migrants into St. Petersburg, Florida reveals that states north of the Mason-Dixon Line and east of the Mississippi River contribute many more retirees to the migration stream than do nearby states. General population movements more frequently terminate in neighboring states with short distance moves predominating. Although there is a strong north-to-south spatial bias in both elderly and general population movements towards the Sun Belt, there appear to be significant differences in the states which receive these migrants (Flynn, 1978).

Older migrants also differ from non-migrant elderly. Elderly migrants have higher incomes and educational levels, are more likely to be white and in better health than non-migrants. Their preretirement homes are more likely to be found in the suburbs than in other parts of metropolitan areas or in rural areas, and couples are more likely to move than single individuals.

Unfortunately, no published study describes the spatial pattern of elderly migration. This is primarily because of data limitations; either the observations are limited to small numbers of people in a particular case study, or to net migration rates that obscure the spatial pattern of migrant origins and destinations. If we examine 1970 census data, the Public Use Sample (1/100), we can identify the volume of elderly migration that occurred during the period 1965 to 1970 between every pair of states and compile a map, Figure 11, of these movements. For purposes of generalization, we have excluded many of the smaller state-to-state flows from the map. Very large volumes of interstate migration occur between northeastern states and coastal or southern states such as Florida, Arizona, Oregon, California, and Texas. In fact, by including Arkansas these six states account for more than 50 percent of all elderly interstate in-migration. Northeastern states, New York, Pennsylvania, Ohio, Illinois, and Michigan account for nearly 50 percent of all elderly migration origins. Figure 11 shows a fairly restricted general pattern of elderly migration with the bulk of movement occurring between a small number of states.

The major destination states are those which most people would consider well endowed with scenic, recreational, and other amenities. As might be expected these states are highly attractive to elderly migrants, especially to those who have recently retired (Figure 10).

Closer examination of the patterns reveals considerable spatial variation in migration streams, i.e., all flows which terminate in a specific state. For example, the Florida stream is comprised primarily of elderly who are relocating from states in New England and eastern portions of the midwest, whereas the California stream draws primarily from central states and the west coast. On the other hand, the Washington-Oregon stream attracts large numbers of migrants from only nearby states. Major elderly migration streams can be classified as either national or regional. California and Florida, as well as Arizona, can be classified as national destinations because they attract migrants from long distances and from a considerable number of states, whereas Arkansas, Washington, Oregon, New Jersey, and Texas represent major regional destinations characterized by shorter distance migrations from surrounding states.

Both national and regional streams have a considerable impact on the destination communities in restructuring the demographic composition of destination communities. For example, in 1950 Arkansas ranked 21st among all states in its percent of elderly population relative to the state total but had moved to second position in 1970, primarily as a reslt of elderly in-migration. As was noted in the last chapter, Florida increased its proportion of elderly residents by 25 percent during the period 1965 to 1970. Thus, despite the relatively low proportion of all older persons who engage in long distance migration, the spatial concentration of migration destinations results in disproportionately large impacts. Although little documentation exists of these impacts in other than demographic terms, it is logical to expect that there are significant impacts on local economies and on the provision of social services.

The long term implications and impacts of these migration patterns may be even more significant given the fact that it is primarily the young-old who engage in interstate migration and the old-old who require most assistance. The young-old who migrate to a retirement community shortly after retirement have the financial, health, and other resources necessary to support that migration. In time, however, their resources can be expected to decline. It is likely, then, that communities which happily embrace and often actively recruit elderly migrants may later find themselves experiencing considerable problems. For example, recent stories in the popular media indicate that Miami's convention business is waning because of its image as a geriatric center. Additionally, critics charge that current fiscal problems are partly the result of earlier massive elderly migration. Clearly, there is an urgent need for research into the community impacts of elderly migration.

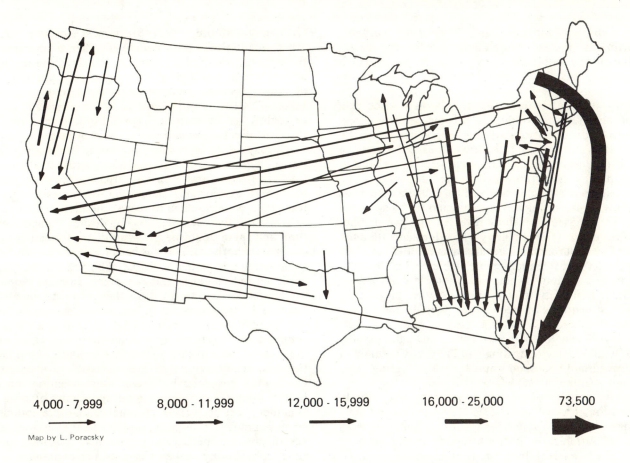

Figure 11. U.S. interstate migration of persons age 60 and over, 1965–1970. Calculated from U.S. Bureau of the Census, *1970 Public Use Sample (1/100)*.

Local Patterns of Residential Change

A commonly held stereotype of local residential change by older people portrays movements from a single family home into either an inner-city apartment or a nursing home. Actually, very few older people are institutionalized at any time, i.e., approximately four percent (U.S. Bureau of the Census, 1976a) and, as will be shown, relocation to the city's center is quite uncommon. We shall also see that this area has not been heavily studied despite the fact that local moves occur much more frequently than long distance migrations. In keeping with demographic convention, local movements will be referred to simply as relocation, reflecting the view that movements over short distances are less disruptive than long distance moves, and therefore, constitute a distinct form of migration behavior.

One of the earliest geographical studies of elderly relocation (Golant, 1972) compares elderly relocation to that of younger cohorts. Older people were found to be more residentially stable than younger people. The average length of residency in the same home was found to be 18.4 years for the elderly as opposed to 14.2 years for those of later middle age. Elderly widows were more mobile than male household heads. With increased age there was a reduction of elderly household heads living in single family dwelling units (owners), and a corresponding rise in the number of elderly household heads who occupied multiple family units, especially apartments (renters), although a considerable majority still occupied single family homes. Elderly household heads tended to move shorter distances than those in pre-elderly cohorts. The spatial pattern of intraurban relocation was biased away from the central city, and only a small percentage of relocations occurred in the direction of the central city.

Many of these findings were corroborated in an examination of elderly movers in Kansas City, Kansas (Wiseman and Virden, 1977). Approximately 70 percent of the relocations involved movement away from the CBD. Again, most residential change occurred over relatively short distances. Thus, the general pattern of elderly intraurban relocation appears to be one in which the majority of elderly move away from the CBD. This "suburbanization wave" originates in older residential areas located on the fringe of the central city. These moves traverse only short distances and most frequently terminate in older and "nearer" suburban areas of the city. A counter wave of elderly moving into the city's core is not evident despite the common belief that during later stages in the life cycle older people relinquish single family dwelling units in semi-suburban locations and relocate to "urban" apartments. Instead, there is considerable movement of the elderly within the fringes of the inner city which apparently has little directional bias in favor of the CDB.

If we integrate these spatial patterns of relocation with those reported in the last chapter concerning residential concentrations of older persons, it can be seen that intraurban relocation does not result in creating elderly ghettos but rather perpetuates present patterns of concentration within the inner city and its fringes, or contributes to somewhat reduced concentrations by dispersing older people into suburban areas.

The Kansas City study revealed that two distinct profiles characterized elderly who relocated within the city. The suburbanizing group was wealthier, socially more active, residentially more stable, and more apt to be home and auto owners, i.e., middle class suburbanites. Inner-city movers were diverse. In general, they had histories of frequent residential change, low disposable incomes, and low levels of social contact. They were less likely to own homes and automobiles. Nearly all elderly relocation within the city resulted in improved neighborhood status for the relocating older person (Virden, 1976).

Other studies identify the reasons given for elderly relocation. Lawton *et al.* (1973) report that the most frequently cited reasons are: housing and neighborhood dissatisfaction, declining health and the need for assistance, cost of living reductions, a desire to be near relatives, and the desire for improved residential amenities. Nelson and Winter (1975) conclude that the consideration of moving is associated with the occurrence of life disruptive events, low levels of personal independence, and reduced levels of housing and neighborhood satisfaction. These and other studies (Lenzer, 1965; Goldscheider, 1966; and Van Arsdol *et al.*, 1968) are in general agreement as to the general motivations for relocation.

The complex spatial pattern of relocation, the diversity of profiles characterizing relocating elderly, and the many reasons given for relocation combine to make description and understanding of elderly relocation a very difficult task. Perhaps this is why few models of elderly relocation have been developed and tested. The task becomes even more complex when all elderly residential change is addressed including migration. A general model is needed, however, to develop an explanatory theory and to provide a framework that can integrate research findings. The following is an attempt to model the decision making process of older people who change residential locations.

A Model of Residential Change

The decision making process can be viewed as in Figure 12, where the potential migrant (or relocator) responds to stimuli and weighs alternative courses of action. This model incorporates the existing view of residential change as involving two decisions, the decision to move and the decision of where to move (Brown and Moore, 1970). Since most elderly people are residentially stable relative to other segments of the general population, many of the triggering mechanisms which stimulate thinking about the possibility of moving can be grouped under the heading "push factors." Critical life events such as retirement, loss of health, loss of income, or loss of spouse can trigger the consideration of moving. For many older people there may be little if any time spent in deciding to move; they may be forced to relocate because of eviction, fire or natural disaster, urban renewal, or for other reasons. For most people, however, less precipitous factors cause them to reevaluate their residential satisfaction. For example, housing desires change over time and there could be growing dissatisfaction with one's neighborhood, perhaps because of changes in the socio-economic status of the neighborhood that occur while an individual is aging-in-place. In other words dissatisfaction can result from changes in the person, changes in the environment, or both. The successful relocation of a close friend, a fellow worker after retirement, or a relative to a community perceived as more attractive can surely stimulate thoughts of migration. Similarly, the belief that a possible destination community has desirable recreational amenities or a better climate can also encourage such thinking. Whether these triggering mechanisms are precipitous or more gradual influences, it seems likely that several act in concert, perhaps in cumulative fashion over time, contributing to the individual's resolve to move.

The resolve to move can be enhanced or diminished by a number of considerations that might be called facilitating/inhibiting factors. These include: 1) personal resources such as income, self concept, and health; 2) ties to friends and relatives either in the present location or elsewhere; and 3) former migration experience, whether positive or negative.

If the decision is not to move, living conditions may be adjusted by remodeling the home, so that dissatisfaction with the present residential situation is decreased. For some, especially those whose residential mobility is severely constrained and adjustment limited because of income or health, psychological adjustments must be made that will allow them to live with the stress resulting from residential dissatisfaction.

If the result is a decision to move, a search process begins with gathering information about alternative destinations. Several factors are important in this process because the amount and type of information about destination alternatives either expands or restricts relocation options. Former vacation and residential experience can contribute to awareness of possible destinations. For example, Shelley's (1978) recent study of migrants to an Ozark community indicates that a majority of migrants had former vacation or residential experience in the community. In addition, vicarious experience from information gained from friends, relatives and fellow workers can be very influential to the destination selection process.

Very important in this regard, and almost totally overlooked in studies of elderly migration, are the

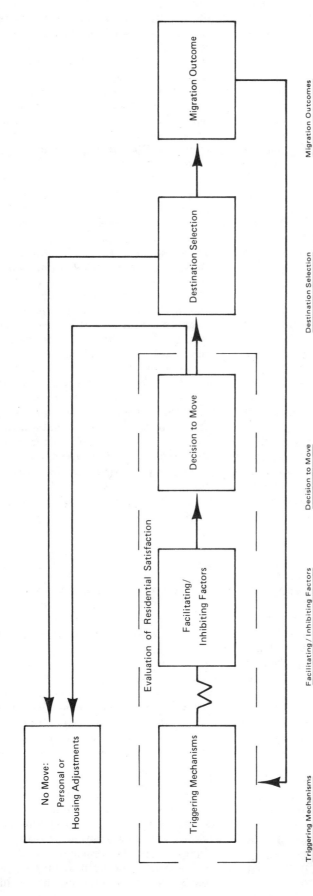

Figure 12. Theoretical model of elderly migration process.

selective recruitment efforts of departments of tourism, developers, chambers of commerce, fraternal organizations, and other community boosters. These groups often get in touch with potential migrants directly and provide information about the community and may offer inducements to visit or move there. For many people this activity might well trigger the consideration of moving at an earlier age than otherwise would be the case and lead them to long-term planning for a retirement move, e.g., buying a vacation or second home. This is especially important in migration to nearby regional retirement centers.

In selecting a destination, still other factors may be influential. For example, the availability of supportive persons or groups within the destination community (especially for interstate migrants) can sway locational considerations. The migrant might have friends, relatives, and church members who help "find a place," or "put one up," "look together," or provide introductions. In a less direct form of support, they might simply reassure the potential migrant through their earlier and successful move.

Although the search process may be unsuccessful and lead to a reconsideration of the decision to move and ultimately to personal or residential adjustments, for those who choose a new location there will be several types of migration outcomes. Those directly affecting the migrant's quality of life include: 1) the community and its location, 2) living arrangements, 3) housing unit type, 4) neighborhood, 5) social network adjustments, and 6) activity and service opportunities. It is likely that different combinations of these outcomes apply to different subgroups of migrants.

Different patterns of decision making and outcomes can be hypothesized for various mover subgroups. For example, local movers are probably more influenced by push factors than migrants. Here, critical life events such as loss of health might necessitate a decision to move, and alternative destinations would be severely limited to those places offering needed assistance. Health care providers or relatives might be influential in the decision to move, and may actually select the final destination. Elderly residents of inner city neighborhoods might experience "forced migration" and thus skip the decision to move portion of the model while focusing all attention on destination selection. Long distance migrants might weigh nearly all of the factors described in the model in ultimately arriving at the selection of a new residence in a retirement community. These examples call attention, once again, to the fact that as a group the elderly are as diverse as any cohort of the population, and it is reasonable to assume that their migration decision making is just as complex, if not more so, than that of the general migrant. To date, studies of elderly residential change have not addressed outcomes adequately or considered variation among elderly subgroups. (For a detailed identification of these subgroups and a consideration of how the process of residential change varies among these groups leading to different outcomes see Wiseman and Roseman, 1979.)

All of the foregoing indicates that many older people are not simply aging-in-place. A large number actively change their environmental setting. Thus, the common stereotype that older people constitute a homogeneous group patiently awaiting the ultimate "move" is inaccurate. Furthermore, not all elderly migrants are moving to Sun City, a famous retirement community in Arizona, or to "God's waiting room," a nursing home. Rather, elderly migration is characterized by complex spatial patterns and a wide range of migration factors.

V. ENVIRONMENT AND AGING

Geographers have long been interested in the relationships that exist between the individual and the environment. Very few have studied these relationships with respect to older people, although they are well quaified to do so. This is unfortunate for two reasons. First, studies in other disciplines demonstrate that the environment directly influences the well-being of older people (Lawton and Cohen, 1974; Lawton, 1975a; Berghorn *et al.*, 1978). For example, after exercising appropriate controls numerous studies have shown that mortality and morbidity rates increase when older individuals change their environmental setting to an institution or even between institutions (Tobin and Lieberman: 1976, 1–24). Second, because older people are more sensitive to environmental influences than most other age groups, they constitute an ideal study population for investigating individual-environmental relationships.

In examining this spatial aspect of aging we begin by defining what we mean by environment. Next, a geographical perspective on individual-environmental relationships is developed. This is followed by a brief review of geographical studies and a presentation of sociogerontological perspectives of individual-environmental relationships. The chapter ends by merging the geographical and sociogeronotological perspectives to provide a framework for further study.

Definitions and Dimensions of Environment

There is diversity among scholars as to definition of the environment and a lack of agreement on methodological approaches to the general study of Man-Environment Relationships (MER). Rapoport (1973) characterizes the field as lacking integration, particularly theoretical orientation. He identifies 12 interrelated areas of study ranging from the development of ecological, ethological, and evolutionary models of MER to studies of preference, perception, choice, adaption, and cognition. Although a few aging studies can be found in several of these areas, the body of literature on Aging Environment Relationships (AER) is small.

Environment can be thought of as being composed of several dimensions among which are physical, psychological, political, social, and cultural. These in turn can be broken down into smaller components depending on the interests and purposes of the researcher. Thus, physical environment may be as broadly conceived as encompassing an entire city's "built environment" or merely one dwelling unit. Because scholars often focus primarily on their own disciplinary dimension, it is difficult to integrate aging MER studies to produce a balanced picture of life experiences in old age as they are related to the environment.

For example, Gubrium (1972), a gerontologist, has elaborated a "socio-environmental theory of aging" that stresses the sociological dimension of the environment. He identifies two "contexts" of environment: the individual and social. The social refers to "the normative outcomes of social homogeneity, residential proximity (spatial aspect), and local protectiveness" (Gubrium, 1973: 76). The individual context includes "those activity resources such as health, solvency, and social support that influence behavior flexibility." He posits that those older people who possess little behavior flexibility (low individual resources) are most sensitive to the environment, especially social norms. For example, older persons with low behavior flexibility living in an environment with a wide range of social situations and norms might feel dissatisfied with themselves and their life situation when what is expected of them by "significant others" in their environment is either more than they can achieve or incongruent with what they expect of themselves. Such a person might be more satisfied in an age homogeneous environment. Although Gubrium focuses upon the social dimension of environment and the need for congruence between the individual's level of resources (behavioral flexibility in this case), implicit in this and many other aging-environment studies are notions that spatial arrangement, i.e., the geographic distribution, density and propinquity of other older people, are important indirect determinants of an older person's pattern of social interaction within the environment.

Thus Michelson (1970), in *Man and His Urban Environment*, argues that space has been used as a *medium* in most of human ecology rather than as a variable with a potential effect of its own. He calls for a systems approach to the study of the environment and identifies five systems that are distinct yet interdependent: social, cultural, psychological, behavioral organism, and environmental. The model he develops stresses the interrelationship of these five systems—each influencing the others—and does not suggest a hierarchical ordering of the systems that would imply some sort of determinism (that is, one system dominating another). An illustration is given of such an interrelationship relevant to family activities (Michelson, 1970: 28):

> The...model is exemplified by studies which show that areas of cities with a high proportion of multiple dwellings and often scattered commercial enterprises are successful in accommodating people who wish to maintain relatively wide kinship networks....working class families living in older, more crowded sections of town depend on a wide range of relatives for recreation assistance, and just plain companionship. They (studies) have followed people from these areas who were subsequently forced to relocate in locations with far different physical characteristics (e.g., 'typical' suburbs), and they then noted an unanticipated, undesired, and unfortunate lessening of extended family activities which could only be explained by environmental factors. In this case, one could suggest that intense family interaction is *congruent* with the physical factors of the former setting and incongruent with that of the latter.

He notes later that suburbia is characterized by a higher number of nuclear families, and consequently there is a greater emphasis on neighboring and friendship networks. At one point, he considers the aged specifically and concludes that most elderly find greatest satisfaction in neighborhoods with a concentration of like-aged people, particularly when they have local life styles.

Whether one focuses upon the social, cultural or other dimensions of environment, it is clear that spatial arrangement of elements within the environment is a major factor in any man-environment study. Michelson's example is eminently spatial because it considers different locations, inner city, and suburbia. Even Gubrium's primary orientation to the social dimension implicitly considers spatial setting attributes such as the number of other older people within a neighborhood. Thus a key element in most man-environment studies is the set of spatial relationships that exist between an individual or group and salient elements within the environment. Such elements might include man-made features of the "built" environment, the location of certain types of activity opportunities, such as parks, stores and churches, or even other people.

Geographical Perspective of Aging Environment Relationships (AER)

The above indicates that greater attention should be paid to spatial aspects of AER. One way to do this is to employ the perspective of spatial interaction. This perspective views the environment as a place that contains the elements comprising the dimensions discussed above. Thus, we might view the environment as presenting opportunities to the individual for obtaining necessities and for potentially enhancing quality of life. At the same time, the environment can confront a person with stressful situations and obstacles to obtaining a satisfying life. Environmental influences on individual behavior can be examined by observing interaction patterns in different environmental settings. To employ this perspective we must define what we mean by spatial interaction and further describe the spatial nature of the environment.

Rowles (1978) identifies four modalities of geographical interaction with the environment: action, orientation, feeling, and fantasy. Action is that physical movement that occurs within the environment. It can be immediate in that it is found in the proximal physical setting of the home or it can be our everyday activity pattern that extends beyond the home into the neighborhood and community. It also includes occasional trips to other communities. Distance and frequency of this type of environmental interaction distinguish specific subcategories of action. Because action is an obvious expression of environmental interaction, most AER studies have focused upon this aspect of geographical environmental experience, such as daily or weekly activity patterns.

A second type of geographical interaction with the environment is orientation, the cognitive differentiation of environmental spaces or places. This is the personal schema employed to organize individually relevant places in the environment. For example, each of us has a mental map of the environment composed of features such as landmarks, activity locations, and travel paths that we organize by a set of spatial relationships. This orientation is important in that we use it to navigate through the environment. Thus, it influences action within the environment.

A third type of environmental experience is that of geographical feeling, that is, the meaning that places in the environment have for us. Our emotional attachment to places can be temporary, permanent, highly personal, or widely shared. It can be a single emotion or span a broad range of feelings. For example, we may develop a wide range of emotional bonds to a neighborhood park that we shared with other neighbors. These feelings may remain even after we relocate to another neighborhood. This is a permanent, shared range of feeling we have for a place in the environment we hold to be important.

Fantasy is a fourth kind of geographical experience with the environment. It is vicarious and can be displaced in both time and space. We engage in geographical fantasy when we think of favorite vacation places. We may be reflecting on an actual former experience or projecting to an anticipated environmental experience.

It is important to develop a geographical conceptualization of the environment. The notions of distance and spatial scale can be employed to identify various environmental spaces. We begin by defining environment as encompassing all space beyond the individual. Based primarily upon increasing distance from home, the focal point of one's activity or environmental interaction pattern, we can identify several zones or spaces within the environment with which we interact in different ways and for different purposes. (See Figure 13.) Home provides shelter, comfort, and security not

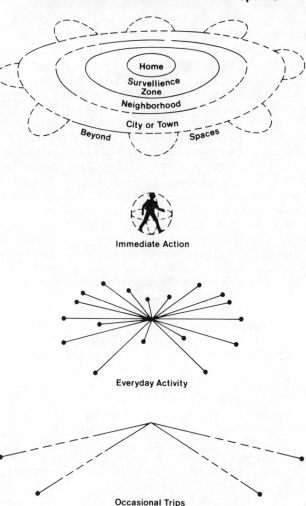

Figure 13. Environmental spaces and levels of action. From Graham D. Rowles, 1978, *Prisoners of Space? Exploring the Geographical Experience of Older People*. Boulder, Colo.: Westview Press, pp. 165 and 172. © Westview Press, Boulder, Colorado, 1978; reprinted by permission.

obtained from other environmental spaces. We may spend much time interacting with the home environment and doing things not done elsewhere. The surveillance zone lies beyond the home and we interact with it less directly, mostly in a visual way. Some people may develop strong emotional attachments with this space and they deeply regret the loss of a tree, the closing of a store, or the loss of a view resulting from the construction of a new house next door. The neighborhood provides opportunities for friendship, socializing, and mutual assistance whereas the city or community provides recreational and entertainment opportunities, places of employment, places from which we obtain life necessities and niceties. Spaces beyond might include places where we vacation, have lived before, or the communities of relatives and friends.

Aging Studies of Spatial Interaction

Most research on environmental interaction outside the home has been directed to examination of older peoples' patterns of action with city or community spaces. Several studies compare interaction frequencies of older people with those of younger adult cohorts. They represent an important step in understanding AER and have contributed directly to programs developed to facilitate environmental interaction, e.g., provision of better transportation services.

The action patterns of older people differ in many ways from those of younger groups. Older people report an overall lower level of trip frequency (Carp, 1971; Markovitz, 1971), although a comparison of trip frequency for all but work trip purposes reveals that the elderly are not much different than pre-elderly (Golant, 1972; Hanson, 1978). There is a difference in modes of transportation used with older people reporting fewer auto trips and slightly more trips by mass transit (Wynn and Levinson, 1967; Marble, Hanson, and Hanson, 1973). Older people apparently travel at different times than other age cohorts, scheduling their trips for off-peak hours (Golant, 1972; Marble, Hanson, and Hanson, 1973). In addition, much of this literature suggests that the spatial extent of the older person's action is more limited than that of younger people. A recent study of people in Uppsala, Sweden reveals that the total distance traveled by the elderly is less than that reported for younger people, (Hanson, 1978). In general, these and other studies reveal that older people, when compared to younger adults, have more restricted patterns of action within the environment.

The significance of this restriction in the lives of older people can be glimpsed from a nationwide survey shown on Table 6 (Harris and Associates, 1975). In all but church or synagogue activities, the elderly reported lower levels of participation: thirty percent had not been to a restaurant within the past year; seventy percent and more had not participated in an entertainment such as going to a movie, library, sports event, concert, or park; and ten percent had not even gone shopping.

Reasons for restricted environmental action patterns of older people have been set forth in many studies, several of which are found in a special report, *Transportation and Aging: Selected Issues* (Cantilli and Shmelzer, 1971), resulting from the 1970 White House Conference on Aging. In general, older people have lower individual resources relating to mobility. They are less likely to be auto owners; they have less disposable income to purchase transportation (and support such activities as shopping and entertainment); and many have physical limitations that make walking or using mass transit difficult.

Nearly all of these studies focus on that portion of the environment which lies beyond a person's neighborhood. Research at the neighborhood scale is also revealing, although fewer studies have been completed.

TABLE 6. COMPARISON OF ACTIVITIES WITHIN THE PAST YEAR

	Total Public 18–64 %	65 and Over %	Net Difference
Places to shop	97	90	−7
The home of a neighbor	92	85	−7
The home of a relative	92	85	−7
A restaurant	91	69	−22
A doctor or clinic	85	82	−3
A church or synagogue	74	77	+3
A movie	70	22	−48
A public park	67	31	−36
A sports event	59	19	−40
A library	52	22	−30
A live theatre, dance or musical concert performance	46	17	−29
A museum	41	18	−23
A community or neighborhood center or recreation center	35	17	−18

Source: Harris and Associates, Inc., 1975:177. Reprinted/excerpted from *The Myth and Reality of Aging in America*, a study prepared by Louis Harris and Associates, Inc., for The National Council on the Aging, Inc., Washington, D.C. © 1975.

Regnier (1974) reports on the neighborhood action patterns and cognitive maps of older people. A study in Los Angeles shows that older people have a strong sense of neighborhood and that its core can be delineated by aggregating mental maps to produce a consensual map. Larger neighborhoods are identified by older people with automobiles, high socioeconomic status, long duration of residence, good health and high activity levels, in other words, people who are very active in the environment. A second study by Regnier (1976) attempts to control for environmental setting especially variation in residential location. By examining shopping activity patterns and use of the neighborhood environment to obtain goods and services he finds that activity patterns are a function of proximity to shopping opportunities, long established behavior (shopping) patterns, the cost of goods and ethnicity as it relates to preference for specific goods (e.g., Chinese food). These studies are also important because they stress the utility of analyzing orientation through the use of mental maps to determine what older people experience in the environment, what they perceive to be important, and what perceptual barriers exist to action within the environment.

The body of literature described above is significant in several respects. It identifies the low mobility resources of older people and the restricted nature of their action within the city or community environment. It indicates the importance of this restricted action and suggests ways to enhance interaction, primarily by increasing the mobility of older people. As a result of such studies several federally sponsored programs have been developed to improve transportation services to older persons. These are described in the next chapter.

However, the bulk of this literature has obvious limitations when placed in the broader context of spatial interaction. It focuses primarily on one environmental space. Although it often compares age cohorts, it seldom, if ever, controls for differences in environmental setting. Few studies disaggregate the elderly population into meaningful subgroups such as those based upon environment setting and level of individual resources.

Other Perspectives of AER

Nearly all work in aging which addresses AER is undertaken at the microenvironmental level, that space which extends from the individual to the limit of what is considered the boundary of the home or residential unit. Environmental psychologists and architects have done most of this research. Although many of the concepts and findings from these studies can be transferred profitably to other levels of environmental study, it is dangerous to engage in wholesale transfer for several reasons. First, we use and interact with different portions of the environment in different ways. For example, although one might argue that going to the refrigerator and the grocery store are similar activities because they share a common purpose, it is apparent that the physical capabilities needed to engage in these activities are very different, as are the frequencies and costs of such activities. Second, most of what we know about the relationships of older people and the micro-environment is based upon studies that examine only a very small proportion of the elderly population, mostly older people found in institutional or public housing settings. The external validity of these research findings have severe limitations so that it is difficult to generalize study results to describe the AER of most elderly people.

Despite these limitations, social gerontologists have developed several noteworthy theories of AER. The three reviewed here are those most widely embraced. The first is an extension of Pastalan's "Age Loss Continuum," described in Chapter II, which views the process of aging as resulting in an expansion and contraction of life space. This might be defined in geographic terms as the spatial extent of one's activity patterns. One gains in mobility and control over the environment during the earliest years of life, experiences a stable level or plateau during the middle period of life, and then loses life space during the latest years because of the continuum of losses.

Figure 14 takes some liberty with Pastalan's exposition for illustrative purposes and infers different hypothetical slopes for the function over various life stages. For example, a child's world or that portion of the environment which children experience and interact with might expand rapidly until into the early school period when spatial interaction patterns become fairly routine. A period of modest expansion might be followed by rapid growth as one's mobility increases

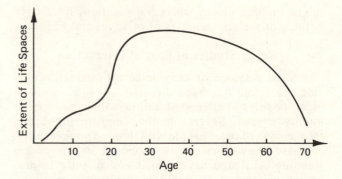

Figure 14. Schematic portrayal of age-loss continuum across the life span.

by obtaining a driver's license, additional income from employment, or residential migration to attend college. According to this theory, the latest years are characterized by a reversal of the process that produces a constriction of life space because of the losses which characterize old age.

This theory is both logically appealing and to some extent empirically substantiated. However, it has several drawbacks. The pattern of gradual expansion and subsequent constriction of life space through the life cycle is subject to significant individual variation. Sex, work status, and socioeconomic status all influence the spatial range of environmental interactions. The results of a recent study of women's leisure activities underline the importance of these individual variations. Contrary to Figure 14, Preston (1978) found that leisure activities were most dispersed among working women who had not yet borne children and older women whose parental responsibilities were ended. During the child-raising periods of the life cycle, women concentrated their activities within the local residential area. Thus, Figure 14 represents the aggregate pattern of environmental interactions throughout the life cycle. At any time, unique personal circumstances alter this pattern.

Furthermore, it seems unlikely that the processes of growth and decline are mirror images. The older person has a wealth of experience and often a tenacious desire to resist the rocking chair. For example, losing a driver's license may appear initially as restrictive to an older person as obtaining a license facilitates movement to a young person, but the older person has several coping strategies. These include, riding with friends, use of public transit, and residential relocation. It is important that future studies focus upon these coping strategies, not only to ascertain if the processes of growth and decline are similar, but also to identify successful strategies that can be taught to older people to mitigate the impact of losses as a result of advancing age.

Several years ago Lawton and Simon (1968) articulated an "environmental docility hypothesis." The hypothesis states that as an individual ages, competence (similar to individual resources) declines and the environment becomes more difficult for the older person. In its narrowest sense this hypothesis would logically follow from Pastalan's theory. Despite the pejorative connotation of the term "docility," Lawton's theoretical thinking does include provision for an active older person and more positive AER.

More recently, Lawton has specified an AER theory that is highly cognizant of interindividual variation and that recognizes the environment as having both a positive as well as a negative influence on the life of an older person (Lawton, 1975a). Rather than focusing on the stress that the environment can place upon the elderly, environmental influences are termed "environmental press." Two types of press are conceived, real press such as relocation to an unfamiliar environment, and perceived press such as that engendered by the possibility of a relocation. This theory is presented graphically in Figure 15. In relating individual competence to various levels of environmental press the theory postulates that the level of individual adaptation (behavior) is surrounded by zones of marginal behavior and ultimately zones of negative affect and maladaptive behavior. Thus, the theory views human behavior as a function of individual competence in the context of environmental press. The emphasis is clearly on adaptive behavior and the theory allows for the inclusion of the total range of adaptive behaviors.

A hypothetical example will help to clarify some of the terms and relationships depicted. Assume that an individual has a given level of competence and is in an environment with a given level of press, position a in Figure 15. Now assume that this individual experiences a stroke and a consequent loss of competence to position b; the level of press is the same and too high for positive adaptive behavior. Therefore, the individual might cope by reducing the level of press through the process of residential relocation, perhaps moving to a residential setting where some care is provided, position c. Here the level of environmental press is well below the individual's level of competence. The person can easily cope with the environment and probably enjoys an environment-competence situation which might be termed maximum comfort. However, if this person recovers fully from all effects of the stroke and regains the original level of competence, the press resulting from the limited care residence is too low for the individual and maladaptive behavior may be manifest, position d. Here another relocation might be warranted, one which results in a healthier balance between the individual's level of competence and environmental stress, location a. Clearly there are levels of environmental press that push us to reach our performance potential just as there are levels of press that cause us to become too comfortable. This theory emphasizes reaching a proper balance between competence and press for each individual.

Lawton identifies possible problems with this theory. For example, neither press nor competence is a unitary characteristic. An individual may be low in biological competence but quite high in sensory and cognitive competence. Similarly, it is difficult to

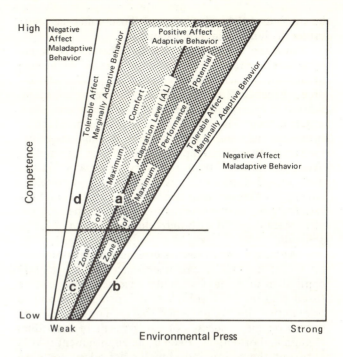

Figure 15. Schematic representation of an ecological model of aging. After M. Powell Lawton and Lucille Nahemov, 1973, "Ecology and the Aging Process," in Carl Eisdorfer and M. Powell Lawton (eds.), *The Psychology of Adult Development and Aging*, p. 661. Copyright, 1973 by the American Psychological Association, Washington, D.C. Reprinted by permission.

characterize the multidimensional environment with a single value. Despite this and other problems the theory is very useful because it recognizes that environmental influences can be positive as well as negative for the older person, and that older individuals vary considerably in terms of competence level.

Another example of a positive approach is found in the theoretical work of Eva Kahana (1975) which, similar to Lawton, describes a theory of environment-individual congruence. Her perspective is strongly prescriptive in that she views old people as having highly individualistic sets of needs and preferences that should be matched to effect congruence with the unique characteristics of specific environments. She identifies several dimensions along which the matching should occur. For example, the individual's preference for change or stability should be matched with the age heterogeneity or homogeneity of the neighborhood or housing environment. Similarly, one's preference for institutional versus individual control should be matched to the amount of one or the other found in the environment. It is relatively easy to see how this environmental perspective could be most useful in developing housing environments for the individual confronting many of the problems of later life. It is more difficult, although not impossible, to envision how this theory could be employed to affect environmental spaces at a scale beyond that of the home or the immediate neighborhood. It appears that studies employing this perspective, even in the city environment, could be most useful to planners and those concerned with urban design for an aging society.

In many ways congruence theory is similar to environmental press theory. Both emphasize well-being or satisfaction with the environment. Kahana's notion of congruence is similar to Lawton's zone of adaptability, i.e., when press equals competence. Congruence theory is useful in that it raises many questions such as what are the relevant dimensions of environment that match individual needs? Or, is a perfect match on all dimensions necessary for satisfaction and well-being? Similarly, press theory calls attention to coping strategies that are employed in achieving satisfaction, perhaps recognizing that a perfect environmental match with individual needs can never be achieved.

Although these theories originate in physiological or social psychological disciplines and are mostly applied in microenvironmental research, they can be fused with the geographer's spatial perspective and be relevant to all environmental spaces. For example, by definition the processes of aging result in individual change and often loss. Even if the environment is held constant the aging individual must adapt to these changes at some point. For some, this adaptation results in constricted activity patterns and limited environmental interaction. Others may employ more active coping strategies (adaptive behavior) by shifting to other modes of transportation or changing the mix of activities undertaken within the environment.

Further Geographic Study of AER

If pressed to articulate the perspective that has directed AER research, many geographers would say that it is one of increasing spatial imbalance between the individual and opportunities within the environment. As an individual ages, mobility and other resources needed for action within the environment decline and make it increasingly difficult for the older person to obtain the things needed to support and enrich life. At the same time, the environment is changing and further exacerbating this imbalance. Many older people by aging-in-place are more removed today than ever before from opportunities within the environment. The decentralization and suburbanization of shopping opportunities in recent decades is just one example of environmental change. Thus, at a time when the environment demands greater mobility, many aging people are suffering mobility reduction. Understandably, restricted activity patterns of older people identified in many studies are a source of great concern and programs developed as a result of such study that enhance the mobility of older people are very important.

However, this paradigm focuses essentially on only one or two of the many spaces that comprise the environment (city or community) and on only one mode of geographical experience (action). By merging the geographical conceptualizations of different environmental spaces and different kinds of spatial interaction with the gerontological theories of environmental press and congruence, we can achieve a broader understanding of AER and can readily identify areas of needed research. For example, the theories of environmental press and congruence call attention to the desirability of matching the needs and resources of older people to their environmental setting. The geographic conceptualization indicates that we must categorize environment into different spaces and modes of environmental experience. We must learn what these spaces provide, mean to older people, and what press results from the various spaces and modes of experience. Is congruence between the individual and each space necessary for a satisfying life or can the modalities of our geographical experience with environmental spaces be substituted to achieve the same outcome?

Rowles' (1978) study indicates that important changes in geographical experience with the environment occur during later life. As the individual ages there is a change in emphasis placed upon the various modalities. As mobility declines and action becomes more limited, proximal environmental spaces become more important. Ultimately there may be a substitution of vicarious (fantasy) experience for more direct (action) experience. Further study is needed to ascertain how this is associated with the other modalities such as orientation and feeling. Do these changes explain why the surveillance zones of older people are so important? Does this result in increased importance being placed upon home and neighborhood and could this explain why so many older people resist residential relocation tenaciously?

Clearly we need to learn more about the importance of environmental spaces and types of spatial interaction in the lives of older people. The following questions demonstrate the academic challenge and practical benefits to be derived from such study.

Can the spaces in an institution or communal living arrangement be designed to substitute meaningfully for environmental spaces enjoyed by older people earlier in life? What elements are important in an older person's surveillance zone and how can this space be designed to enhance the environmental experience of older people, especially those who are no longer ambulatory? Particularly exciting is the need to inventory and identify patterns of geographical orientation and fantasy. How do the mental maps of older people differ from those of other cohorts? How do changes in the individual and environment relate to changing emphases among the modes of geographical experience? Is fantasy the ultimate substitute for action? If changing emphasis is beneficial and necessary given the imperatives of old age, how can we facilitate the process to enrich the environmental experience of older people? By addressing questions such as these, geographers can ultimately develop a theory of AER that will not only broaden our understanding of both AER and MER but also do much to enrich the lives of older people.

VI. ASSISTANCE AND SERVICE DELIVERY

Geographers and other social scientists are becoming increasingly involved in planning and enhancing programs designed to meet the special needs of older people. Although the skills that geographers can contribute are not equally applicable to all aspects of the aging's needs, there are several where geographers have made important contributions. Two of these topics are discussed in this chapter, mobility enhancement through the provision of transportation services and locational criteria for siting elderly housing projects and service delivery centers. Before we present these topics we will consider the evolution and structure of today's service delivery system. The chapter ends by discussing an alternative to present service delivery programs and by articulating areas in which geographic study can be expected to contribute further to enhancing the quality of life experienced by older people.

The Service Delivery System

In 1965, the U.S. government enacted the Older Americans Act which declared society's intent to meet the needs of its older citizens. Title I sets forth the goals of federal policy in this area. It states that all older Americans should have equal opportunity to an adequate retirement income; the best physical and mental health possible without the regard to economic status; suitable housing; full restorative services for those needing institutional care; opportunity for employment without discrimination; retirement in health, honor, and dignity; pursuit of meaningful activities; efficient community services, including low cost transportation; and happiness to be gained from knowledge achieved through research, independence, and the exercise of individual initiative in managing one's own life. Having articulated these goals, the government designed a set of programs and an implementing structure that are set forth in other titles of the Older Americans Act and its amendments. For example, Title II forms the Administration on Aging and charges it with the primary responsibility for administration of the Older Americans Act and its specific programs. In addition, it creates the National Information and Resource Clearinghouse for the Aged which has the responsibility of collecting and disseminating information about older persons. Title II also creates the Federal Council on Aging which acts as an advisory group with the responsibility for reviewing and evaluating programs and for providing a forum and source of information to the public.

Title III is one of the act's most important sections for it establishes state agencies on aging and charges them with creating local or area agencies on aging thereby setting up an hierarchical administrative structure that ties together federal, state, and local administrative agencies dealing with the problems of older persons. Funding for this administrative structure and many of the specific programs designed to meet the special needs of older persons comes directly from the federal government in a formulated "pass-along" procedure. Each state receives one-half of one percent of the total funds available, with the remainder distributed on the basis of the state's percentage of the nation's aged. The federal government pays up to 75 percent of the cost of state planning activities, up to 75 percent of the cost of state programs that are not a part of state plans, and up to 90 percent of the cost of programs that are part of state plans. Thus, states are given the responsibility and resources to plan, administer, and coordinate service delivery programs for older persons within their jurisdictions. The actual agency that delivers services to older persons is found at the local level, the Area Agency on Aging. These "triple A's" are usually multi-county agencies that, with the assistance of an advisory council of older persons, handle the details of the various programs. The basic concept behind this structure is to provide a local community group charged with coordinating efforts of many social welfare programs to assist older people. When necessary they are given funds to deliver specific services to elderly clients. Today, most communities are receiving these funds and are offering to older persons many, if not all, of the special services provided under the various titles of recent amendments to the Older Americans Act.

Of the many programs initiated in this manner, the nutrition program, Title VII, is perhaps the most familiar. Although a "meals on wheels" service is also available, this program provides older persons with a nutritionally sound hot lunch for a minimal contribution at a specific congregate meals site. Because these meals are delivered to older persons at a congregate location rather than to the home, the nutrition sites often serve as the spatial point of service delivery for many other services. Nutrition programs are required to provide other activities. Thus, nutrition sites are often found at multipurpose senior centers that also have social, educational, recreational, and health programs. Frequently, it has been necessary for the area agencies to provide transportation services as well. From this initial structure and core of programs, a wide range of activities and additional services has been added. Thus, a formal network of support exists that offers services at designated geographic locations.

In addition to the programs enacted and supported by the federal government, there are several programs providing services to older people that are run exclusively by older people themselves. For example, the Service Corps of Retired Executives (SCORE) is a voluntary organization of retired businessmen and women who assist owners of small businesses with management problems. Other programs include "Green Thumb" that employs older people on a part-time basis in conservation programs and local community improvement efforts in rural areas. This program is funded by the National Farmers Union. The Senior Companion Program is similar to the Foster Grandparents Program, which employs low-income older people to provide individual care to children who reside in institutions. In addition, the Retired Senior Volunteer Program (RSVP) provides a vehicle for older people to volunteer their services in meeting a variety of community needs. Besides providing transportation services, these volunteers often assist in schools, hospitals, day-care centers, and nursing homes. Such programs show that older people can, indeed, help other older people, and the large number of volunteers engaging in these activities testifies to a broad desire among the older population to remain productive members of society.

Obviously, a broad range of programs and activities exists to address the specific needs of older persons. However, when one looks more closely at the distribution of facilities and the actual service delivery programs in place throughout the United States, there still appears to be a considerable gap between need and delivery. For example, Taietz's recent (1975) study demonstrates that rural settings, where significant numbers and certainly large proportions of older people reside, are much less well endowed with service delivery programs than are urban settings. It is possible, although as yet untested, that older people residing in small, rural communities must rely more heavily on informal support networks and relatives and friends than on the formal provision of specific services. Many also believe that some older people most in need of the special services available to them are not participating in programs designed to meet their needs. One of the reasons for this may be that older people feel the stigma of "social welfare recipient" attached to certain highly visible programs. In other cases, older people may be simply unaware of the services available to them. Unfortunately, in still other cases, we see poorly designed and administered programs.

It is also appropriate that we examine transportation needs and programs for the elderly. These needs and programs reveal problem areas that geographers can study and thereby contribute to alleviating hardships that confront older people.

Transportation Services

Ideally, transportation systems should provide continuous access and egress. However, most public transportation systems provide only periodic service throughout the day and sometimes at night. Others have little or no weekend or holiday service or are characterized by long waits for service. Waiting a half hour or more for the next bus, especially in inclement weather, can be physically exhausting or cause considerable inconvenience if one must leave home an hour earlier than usual to meet a doctor's appointment. The design of most systems is to achieve a desirable balance between convenience and cost. Financial constraints and the realities of the mass transit market often dictate defining convenience in terms of the job commuting public. This also results in transit routes that focus on the downtown, the most convenient area for many commuters but inconvenient for the older person who must transfer, possibly several times, to reach a non-work destination.

In order to use conventional mass transit, the rider must be able to travel to the pickup point, be there at the right time, recognize the proper vehicle, board unassisted in a normal length of time, pay the fare, deal with other passengers, find a seat or stand for the trip, endure the jostling and sudden stops and starts often encountered, recognize the proper stop, disembark from the vehicle in a timely fashion, and incur additional travel to the final destination point. From what we already know about many older people, it is clear that they will encounter several difficulties. Walking many blocks to the pickup point can create an obvious hardship and inhibit one's use of public transportation. Problems with visual acuity in old age can impede one's ability to recognize the proper vehicle and identify the desired destination point. Other health problems can make boarding and disembarking a severe difficulty. For many older people, paying the fare adds still another barrier to their mobility. The riding conditions themselves are often difficult because of problems in keeping one's balance and remaining physically stationary in the tumultuous conditions of the vehicle. In addition, fear of crime can be a major deterrent to using conventional transit.

Three major approaches to solving the mobility problems of older people have been attempted (Golant, 1976b): reduced fare and fare free programs, redesign of mass transit systems, and special transportation services. Reduced fare programs exist in nearly all cities that have public transportation systems. This has been done in an attempt to meet the needs of elderly people who have been isolated because of the inability to pay for transportation services and, perhaps not incidentally, to increase demand for public transportation during off-peak hours. (Reduced fare programs are mandated if a transit system received DOT Urban Mass Transit Administration funding from Section III or V programs). Many communities now offer senior citizen discounts of 30 to 50 percent off the regular fares during certain hours of the day and during weekends. In a few instances, these programs have been expanded to cover all hours of the day.

On the surface such programs appear to be highly attractive in meeting the mobility needs of older people, but when one thinks of the many other mobility barriers that confront older persons in using conventional mass transportation systems, it is apparent that this program alone is not sufficient to meet the needs of most older people. Hodge and Schold (1977) analyzed the impact of a reduced fare "pass" program in Seattle and found that participation rates by older persons vary considerably throughout the city. Many older people who need increased mobility were either unaware of the program or, for a variety of reasons,

TABLE 7. PER CAPITA TRIPS PER WEEK

	Frequency		
Trip Purpose	Riders	All Non-Riders	Matched Non-Riders#
Shopping	1.59	2.09*	1.00*
Personal Business	.90	1.00*	.42*
Entertainment–Recreation	.03@	.86@	.08@
Visit Friends and Relatives	.54	1.13*	.54
Church	.40	.60*	.27
Clubs	.14	.44	.08@
Just to Walk or Ride	.26	.44	.15@
Out-of-Town	.61	.22	.08
Medical	.32	.27*	.11*
Total	4.79	7.05	2.73

*Significant difference when compared to ridership group via Chi Square test at 0.05 level of confidence.

#Subset of non-riders selected to match socio-economic and mobility characteristics of riders.

@Distribution of frequency data too restricted to calculate Chi Square statistic. Calculated by author; for further discussion see: Wiseman, 1976.

were unable to participate. Many neighborhoods containing large numbers of older people who probably have severe mobility problems had very low participation rates.

In conjunction with reduced fare programs, local jurisdictions are now paying greater attention to overcoming other transportation barriers that prevent many of the handicapped and elderly from using conventional transit systems. Changes in bus design have been effected to afford the wheelchair user and other persons with restricted ambulatory ability more satisfactory access. Buses that "kneel" to curb level for easier access and egress exist. Entrances are being redesigned to provide easier access. Signs and vehicle markings have been enlarged and redesigned to communicate more effectively often via graphic symbols. These and other changes are enhancing the mobility of elderly people who have available to them a mass transit option.

However, most transit systems are constrained to servicing fixed routes that serve only a limited portion of the urban environment. Many communities, especially those with less than 50,000 people, have no public transportation at all. Some communities are developing special transportation systems. An example is the demand responsive transportation system known as "dial-a-ride" which provides door-to-door service. Two types of systems have been developed. The first requires advance reservation to allow routing and schedules to be developed in advance of actual service delivery so that one unit can service several people on a particular run. This type of service is cost efficient and quite effective especially in areas that have moderate demand densities. Here the cost per trip of providing transportation service is not prohibitively expensive and the quality of service provided is quite high. Wiseman's (1976) study which attempted to measure the impact of such a transportation system on the mobility levels of older people revealed that trip frequencies of the people who used such a system were significantly higher than a similar subgroup of the elderly population that did not use the service (See Table 7). Riders reported twice as many trips outside the home on a weekly basis, and significantly higher trip frequencies for medical visits, shopping, and personal business than the matched group of non-riders.

A true dial-a-ride system is more immediately responsive to demands, i.e., the unit is dispatched immediately upon receipt of a request for services. This is often much more expensive and, if demand is high, can be difficult to operate. In many ways such a system is indistinguishable from taxi service. In fact, recently taxi service has been employed and subsidized to meet the transportation needs of older people in many communities, e.g., Dade County, Florida and Danville, Illinois. Taxi service is most responsive to mobility needs, can provide additional individual attention when necessary, and utilizes transportation services available in the private sector. Its primary disadvantages are the inability to serve nonambulatory persons and in some settings its high service cost. Obviously, in a large city, the provision of taxi service to older persons for all possible trips is a very expensive undertaking. In some situations, especially where such service exists and relatively light travel demand densities exist, subsidized taxi service may be most cost efficient when one compares total cost including equipment and management. Most communities that subsidize taxi service to older persons do so on a limited basis, sometimes restricting the number of subsidized trips or the amount of subsidy permitted in the course of a month. Many also limit service use by issuing tickets or boarding passes. An interesting variation in this approach is being employed by the TRIP program serving a portion of West Virginia that allows patrons to purchase tickets at reduced rates depending on their economic situation. Patrons purchase tickets like food stamps and can "spend" them in similar fashion on different systems operating within the service area, including intercity bus lines.

Enhancing the mobility of the elderly is an area in which geographers have played a significant role since the problem in its abstract form is that of getting people from one place to another. The problem becomes very complex when we realize that older people reside in many different locations and desire to travel to many other locations. A further complication results from the fact that the most effective and convenient systems, dial-a-ride and taxi, are very expensive and there is seldom enough money available to fund such services on an unlimited basis. Thus, an important trade-off exists between cost and effectiveness. Researchers must make careful studies of alternative systems in each community setting and consider mobility needs, the spatial arrangement of the community, and political and economic realities. In situations such as apartment complexes, where large numbers of older people reside at one place and wish to travel to one or two particular places such as downtown or a shopping center, mass transit or special bus service can be employed, sometimes with an economic profit. Similarly, in many neighborhoods with large numbers of older people, where travel demand is high a conventional, fixed-route bus system might be both effective and highly cost efficient. However, in settings where older people are (residentially) dispersed, a demand responsive system might be best and less expensive, because fixed-route, regularly scheduled systems may have high overhead costs. The cost per trip for different systems can range from $3.50 to $7.50 for typical passenger trips of 7–10 miles in rural areas, to $1.20 to $1.40 for typical passenger trips of 2–3 miles in urban areas (U.S. DHEW, AOA, 1975). In areas with very light demand densities, especially rural areas, a modified dial-a-ride system that provides service on a less-than-daily basis might be best.

A considerable body of literature now exists to aid in the analysis and development of these systems (U.S. DHEW, AOA, 1975; and see, for example, McKelvey and Dueker, 1974). However, many issues await further study. For example, some large urban areas have several systems and are concerned about problems of competition (McKelvey and Lichtenheld, 1975). Study must be undertaken to integrate systems so that service is enhanced, not duplicated, and that cost efficiencies are effected. Similarly, there is a need to interface urban and rural systems. Even in a community where a system is well established there is a continual need for monitoring and review so that modifications can be made to increase effectiveness or reduce costs. A dial-a-ride system might be modified to include regularly scheduled runs between points with many trip origins and many trip terminations. Appointments at a medical clinic can be scheduled at common times, and shopping excursions can be planned on certain days. In these cases trips can be collected by dial-a-ride and transferred to a larger unit to yield additional economies of operation.

More study also must be devoted to identifying travel demand and needs. In planning a system and later evaluating its performance it is important to know how much service is demanded, who needs the service, and where this need exists. Survey research, such as conducting door-to-door interviews, is very expensive and usually overestimates demand for a new system in an area where none currently exists (Popper *et al.*, 1976). On the other hand, quantitative attempts (see Burkhardt and Lago, 1976) to model demand often lack relevant data and underestimate "latent demand," needs and demands not being met by present service and trips that would be taken if service (or better service) was provided (Miller, 1976). Planners can also learn about demand in the process of providing service by observing travel behavior patterns. Here we need research to determine how travel patterns relate to quality of life insofar as we can measure it.

Obviously, mobility problems are very prevalent among the elderly, and although society is increasingly attending to those needs and researchers have learned much about addressing this problem, we still need more studies to insure that needs are being met effectively and efficiently.

The Location of Services

Most programs for older people provide service from one or more sites or places in the environment. Proximity to the site and perceived convenience of location (s) are very important in determining the real availability of service. When service is inaccessible it is either underutilized or someone must pay for transportation costs and inconvenience. The proper siting of facilities such as congregate meal sites and senior centers is an essential aspect of efficient and meaningful service delivery. Although many service facilities are already "in place," their locational efficiency should be reevaluated periodically. Other facilities, such as the 300 new rural health centers recently proposed by President Carter, have yet to be situated within the environment and therefore provide an excellent opportunity for application of geographic analysis. Issues of accessibility, spatial efficiency, and "best" location are also inherent in selecting sites for low cost and limited care housing.

We can gain some direction for these studies from research on locational criteria for siting elderly housing projects. Niebanck (1965) asked managers of housing projects to report "satisfactory" distances from an older person's residence to various facilities and found that only a very limited distance, three blocks, is acceptable to most older people for frequent activities, as is shown in Figure 16. However, older people themselves were not contacted and the use of "satisfactory distance" is less useful in planning than would be "maximum distance" or "critical distance." Newcomer (1975) gathered data from 575 older people residing in 154 projects and demonstrated that use of services falls off dramatically with increased distance. However, the study was flawed by the fact that the distances employed were limited to three categories and spatially to 10 blocks. Furthermore, the study did not examine actual use patterns; rather people were asked for hypothetical use-distance information.

The service center siting problem has been only lightly researched as has the importance of proper siting to service delivery and client use patterns. We do not know precisely what the criteria for proper siting are and how to identify the best locations. The problem has characteristics of classical public facility location problems and could be addressed appropriately by geographers trained in locational analysis (Abler *et al.*, 1971; Rushton *et al.*, 1973). In addition, the relationship between use of service and distance from service center should be examined (Newcomer, 1975). Now that most communities have service centers the opportunities to conduct this study are plentiful.

A New Program for Meeting Old Needs

Improving the quality of life for the elderly is an endeavor that demands further attention. The programs of today must be reexamined constantly to insure their relevance, efficiency, and effectiveness. They must also be weighed against alternative courses of action and future needs.

For example, the concept of mobile services is an alternative to the present form of service delivery that is receiving attention and warrants further investigation. This alternative would deliver services to people at their place of residence rather than bringing the people to services. The idea is not new when one thinks of the peddlers, tinkers, and traders of the past as they roamed the countryside bringing wares to people. In recent decades mobile services have declined nearly to the point of non-existence. The milkman, vegetable vendor, and home delivery of groceries are things of the past. Although Meals on Wheels and "Homemaker" assistance are available to older people in many communities, most other goods and services can be obtained only by leaving home. It is intriguing to think of commercial, social, and health services delivery to the homes of older people. Would it not be possible to equip a large truck to provide these services at a variety of convenient neighborhood locations? Would it be

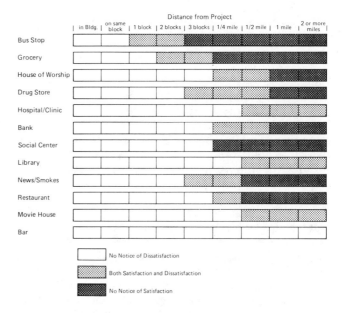

Figure 16. Relative satisfaction of the elderly with the distance from their building to necessary facilities. From Paul L. Niebanck, 1965, *The Elderly in Older Urban Areas: Problems of Adaption and the Effects of Relocation.* Philadelphia, Pa.: University of Pennsylvania, Institute for Environmental Studies, p. 65. Used by permission from the Institute for Environmental Studies, University of Pennsylvania.

possible for such a unit to operate at a profit or at least to decrease public sector subsidy for providing services?

Exploring the potentialities of this concept would require several types of studies. The financial feasibility of such service would have to be established. Estimates of demand would have to be balanced against estimates of service delivery cost. Neighborhoods of high need and demand would have to be identified and the spatial configuration of such a system would have to be designed. The reaction of people to this system would have to be tested in a demonstration program. The idea is exciting not only because it would expand present delivery systems but also because it would make the system more flexible in meeting the needs of older people in the future, particularly the near future when many older people will live in suburban environments (Golant, 1975; 1978).

The next chapter describes some of the changing characteristics of older people themselves and changes in the condition of life older people will experience in the future. Planning to meet the future needs of the elderly is a challenging endeavor that demands innovative ideas and a considerable amount of further research.

VII. "WILL YOU STILL LOVE ME WHEN I'M SIXTY-FOUR?"

The spatial aspects of aging discussed in the preceding chapters represent some of the fields in which geographers are contributing to a better understanding of older people. These are important topics which in some cases directly influence the well-being of older people. As we have seen, knowledge of these topics is incomplete and many questions remain unanswered.

Rather than review what has already been presented, let us briefly consider the future of our aging society. One day most of us will be old. What will older people be like then? What will be changed and what do we need to study to prepare for the future?

Although little rigorous study describes what the future may hold for older people, there is an emerging research literature on the subject. A 1975 special issue of the *Gerontologist* entitled, "Aging in the Year 2000" contains one of the most comprehensive discussions to date. It considers the increasing numbers of older persons, their uses of time and money, residential patterns, mental health, as well as a variety of social and health service needs. It addresses critical issues and underscores the importance of planning now for the decades ahead.

The Aging of Society

The number of older people in the U.S. is increasing dramatically. By the year 2000, estimates indicate that the population age 65 and over will number 26.5 million given present mortality rates, and could be as high as 35 million with a reduction in those rates because of major medical breakthroughs. However, Brotman (1977: 208) cautions that:

> while such a medical advance would have a large impact on life expectancy in the upper ages, the chances are that the startling claims of added years and added numbers in the population literature would not be achieved in full, since death is a result of multiple risks; some people who would not die of cancer at some given age still die from a variety of other causes.

Surprisingly, one of the most fundamental geographical questions that we can ask about this future aged population has not received much attention—where will older people be found? Golant (1975) considers this question and predicts continued growth of elderly populations in metropolitan areas and the warm "retirement" states. The elderly of the future will be concentrated in a variety of settings which in turn will be dispersed across wide areas. Older populations will be both age-segregated and age-integrated, depending on the scale of observation employed. Although we can expect the pattern of nation-wide concentration of elderly persons to be more diffused in the near future, the process of aging-in-place and elderly migration will continue to produce high concentrations of older persons in specific localities. We are now witnessing developments such as local retirement communities, apartment and condominium complexes designed especially for older persons, and publicly subsidized housing projects for the elderly. Golant is optimistic about such developments for the very concentration of older persons can be expected to concentrate demand for transportation and other services in these settlements. This will make obvious the need for services and will reduce the per unit cost of service delivery.

An important change in the near future is that the bulk of the urban elderly will reside in suburban locations, primarily because of the aging-in-place of present population structures. Acknowledging the importance of suburbanization, Golant (1975: 19) looks to the future: "The geometrics of suburban growth will result in an older population that is spatially dispersed over an increasingly larger geographic area." How well can a person live in an environment that is designed for automobile travel when one can no longer operate an automobile? Will society be willing to pay the costs of providing transportation services in an environment which by virtue of its design makes public mass transit extremely expensive? What will those neighborhoods be like in terms of services and special facilities for the aged? Residential environments designed for mobile, young families will have to undergo considerable change in order to provide salubrious environments for older adults. The alternative is that older adults will have to relocate. If this is the case, how will a society comprised primarily of very small family units or single individuals use the housing stock and built environment designed for a different lifestyle?

Housing policy will be a significant determinant of future locational patterns of older people at the local level. The desire to maintain residential independence is strong and several policy options have been suggested to facilitate this. One idea is "negative rent" that would allow the older person to divest accumulated property value over time. Although presently many legal restrictions exist and there is a considerable lack of interest on the part of the financial community to adopt this procedure, essentially this plan would allow the older person to sell a home to a financial institution, but continue living on the property until death or relocation to a nursing home, while receiving monthly payments over a period to be established by examination of actuarial tables. Thus, an older person would no longer have to relocate in order to realize a return on the accumulated investment in the property. This plan would substantially reduce the estate that children might receive, but it would also provide concomitant release from the obligation to provide for one's parents in their old age. This plan would provide many older people with more money, thus reducing the impending social security payments crisis. It would also reduce relocation rates for older people. However, it would impede the "filtering" process which currently operates in the housing market, and there would be many more cases of one to two older persons occupying a very spacious home capable of housing more people. Some view this as an alarming prospect, given that we have now and expect to have in the future a general housing shortage.

An alternative concept is the idea of "shared housing." Here, older people who are presently "overhoused" would be encouraged and assisted to remodel the housing unit in order to share the space with other people, especially older persons. Although the general attitude among older persons toward this notion has not been assessed, it is clear that such a plan would offer many advantages. Older persons would have less difficulty paying property taxes and maintaining large, older homes. The community would experience some relief from local housing shortages and could receive greater revenue from increased property taxes. On the other hand, the zoning codes in most communities that restrict the development of multi-family units in single family residential areas would have to be modified carefully.

The spatial impacts of these ideas must be assessed. Would such programs lead to greater local concentrations of older people? Is it desirable to have an age segregated society reinforced by spatial concentration and separation? Would the environmental setting of older people be enhanced? Would the need for special services increase or diminish? Where would those most in need be located?

Changing Characteristics of Older People

Certainly the prospect of an aging society poses many important questions that demand a better understanding of the spatial aspects of aging. But, changes in the locational patterns of older people represent only a portion of the impacts we can expect from an altered demographic structure. Several important characteristics of the older population can be expected to change in the very near future. This, too, will raise significant policy issues and demand further research on older people and aging.

The financial situation of older people will improve as a result of continuing adjustments in social security laws, pension funds, and other sources of old-age income. However, with larger numbers of retired people, and a continuing trend for many people to retire at an earlier age, there will be more discussion of the nature of the dependency ratio—the relationship of the "dependent groups," both young and elderly, to the middle, working segment of the population. Our society has been willing to invest enormous sums of money into education and programs for the young. Will it be as willing to support those at the other end of the age continuum? Obviously, the question is colored by the fact that although most old people may not be working, they will also have investments and other sources of income that actually represent productive involvement in the economy. With more people living longer, what special services and facilities will have to be provided to support these people in a dignified and satisfying life? And who will pay? What are our obligations to those who have labored in the past?

In the future older people will also be better educated. Bernice Neugarten (1975) predicts that by 1990, the "young-old" will usually be high school and often college graduates. Educational differences between younger and older generations will be smaller than at present, thus reducing many of the disadvantages the current older generation experiences. Higher educational levels are generally associated with higher rates of residential mobility. This suggests that migration rates will increase. Will the "Sun City" stereotype of today become a reality tomorrow?

Higher educational attainment can also be expected to contribute a new meaning to leisure time and the period of retirement.

There are presently experiments with "gradual retirement." These permit an individual to ease out of a position rather than make an abrupt break. The proposed changes in mandatory retirement laws would allow some individuals to continue working well into old age, although few expect that this would be a widespread trend. Rather, we can expect to see earlier retirement for most people. Does this mean that the very definition of old age will change, since so much of it is now tied to retirement? Will attitudes toward work and leisure be modified so that the status of not working loses its negative connotation? How will this affect patterns and the definition of preferred residential environments?

Although retirement is a crisis shared by most older people, males experience its most obvious impacts today because there are low proportions of working females in the present elderly cohort. This, too, will change in the future. It seems likely that the present trend towards women working and having careers will be intensified. Thus, in the future the trauma of retirement may be shared more widely by women. Present trends such as delaying marriage, and for some women not marrying at all, may also modify other crises of old age such as widowhood.

Older people in the future, then, will be more affluent, better educated, healthier, longer-lived, and earlier to retire. Sex role differences will be less pronounced and the very meaning of old age might change. Retirement could be transformed into a time for second careers and a wide variety of creative pursuits.

The aging of society coupled with the changing character of older people will dramatically affect many of our social institutions, such as the family. Considerable research indicates that, contrary to popular conceptions, family connections and support remain significant to older people. Not only do the elderly depend on relatives, they, in turn, are frequently called upon for assistance, particularly by offspring. The nature of the relationship between the old person and kin will vary according to such factors as ethnicity and socioeconomic status, but the family remains a viable unit in modern society. Studies of the general population indicate that although families may live at greater distances from one another than in the past, transportation and communication networks enhance regular contact, and, as we have seen, older people desire to be located near their children.

Sussman (1976) suggests that the modern family has undergone a change in function in response to present needs. Today, he argues, family units act as mediators or buffers between individual members and bureaucratized services provided for that individual and the family often provides the physical link to those services. He suggests that this role will be enhanced in the future.

What could change, and perhaps is already changing, is the nature of the family. What will be the consequences of increasing divorce and remarriage rates? Indeed, what constitutes a "family," a married couple with offspring or a group of mutually concerned old people committed to caring for one another? This latter question bears directly on future policies. What types of living arrangements and household organizations will be eligible for services and assistance? Frequently cited examples of the incompatibility of policy with present standards are those social security regulations that make it economically advantageous for two people to live together without marrying. It is astounding to think that our society could place an economic disincentive on an institution so respected as marriage. For many of today's elderly this results in an extremely difficult and uncomfortable situation which violates life-long values. Which will change—policy or social standards?

Another factor that will contribute to the fostering of different types of family and social structures is the necessity to provide alternatives to institutionalization. The federal government is currently investigating "informal support systems," the majority of which are family assistance to older persons. Some people have suggested that we are already exceeding tolerable levels of government expenditure for social security, housing, and special services. They argue that families will have to resume greater responsibility for aged members in the future. If this does become a social imperative, it is reasonable to assume that our society will have to endorse legislation favorable to family based assistance to the elderly. Adding to the plausibility of these predictions is the likelihood that the older person in the future may have more relatives upon whom to rely as a result of both increased longevity and greater numbers of older persons. Four and even five generation families will not be uncommon. We may soon see the "old-old" relying on their "young-old" children.

Future Study of Aging

Obviously, there is much to think about and plan for as we travel into the future. However, it is also imperative that we carefully examine the present, for by affecting the present we direct the course of the future. Geographers can play a truly significant role in this endeavor. Each of the spatial aspects of aging considered in this paper identifies questions that we will seek to answer by future research.

It is also important that geographers involved with aged studies go beyond the rather limited scope of research suggested here, joining forces with non-academicians as well as researchers from other disciplines, to inject our studies with more meaning and relevance to the lives of older people. For example, studies which focus upon the locational aspects of today's elderly population could also examine the meanings of different locational settings to older people's lives. Research in other disciplines describes only some of the impacts that result from living in age-concentrated versus age-homogeneous housing complexes and neighborhoods. Similarly, study of elderly migration patterns and processes should focus more attention on the outcomes of a change of residential setting. Is the quality of life experienced by older people better after they move? Would many of these people have preferred not to relocate and, if this is true, how could society assist them so that they are not forced to move?

At the same time, students of aging who wish to work in applied fields should be mindful of the potential academic and theoretical implications of their research findings. For example, studies of travel behavior and activity patterns are often undertaken to provide transportation services. These studies also can reveal much about changes in spatial behavior that attend the aging process, and especially the impact of various environmental settings on the lives of older people. Perhaps greater emphasis should be placed upon changing environmental settings of the elderly rather than facilitating their adaptation to changes in the environment.

It is also important that in studying older people we consider what studies of aging can contribute to the discipline of geography. What we learn about older people should be placed into larger historical and societal frameworks. For example, research into the local residential relocation behavior of older people might add much to our limited knowledge about the effects of forced migration on the general population as well and the types of adaptive behaviors that occur during and after a move. Similarly, knowledge gained about the migration behavior of older people can be used to speculate upon future migration patterns of other segments of the general population. In the future we can expect earlier retirement, diminishing ties to employment opportunities, and greater concern with the quality of life. These are the chief characteristics of today's elderly migrants. What do studies of aging migration teach us about the future implications of these and other contemporary trends?

Finally, by studying older people we gain a new awareness of the developmental perspective of aging. Perhaps, here more than anywhere else, the study of aging can enrich other spheres of geographical knowledge. What implications does this perspective hold for the theory and models of human geography? How does spatial behavior change over the course of life? Do the meaning and use of environmental spaces change throughtout life? How important is fantasy experience? How is the surveillance zone used? Do younger age groups also prefer age homogeneous residential environments? Clearly, the discipline of geography can profit from aging research just as aging studies and older people can benefit from the attention of geographers.

BIBLIOGRAPHY

Abler, Ronald, John S. Adams, and Peter Gould, 1971, *Spatial Organization—The Geographer's View of the World.* Englewood Cliffs, N.J.: Prentice-Hall.

Atchley, Robert C., 1972, *The Social Forces in Later Life: An Introduction to Social Gerontology.* Belmont, Calif.: Wadsworth.

———, 1975, "The Life Course, Age Grading, and Age-Linked Demands for Decision Making," in Nancy Datan and Leon H. Ginsberg (eds.), *Life-Span Developmental Psychology: Normative Life Crises.* New York: Academic Press.

Baltes, Paul B., Steven W. Cornelius, and John R. Nesselroad, "Cohort Effects in Developmental Psychology," in J. R. Nesselroad and P. B. Baltes (eds.), *Longitudinal Research in the Behavioral Sciences: Design and Analysis.* New York: Academic Press (forthcoming).

Barsby, Steve L., and Dennis R. Cox, 1975, *Interstate Migration of the Elderly.* Toronto: Heath-Lexington.

Berghorn, Forrest J., Donna E. Schafer, Geoffrey Steere, and Robert F. Wiseman, 1978, *The Urban Elderly: A Study in Life Satisfaction.* New York: Allenheld and Osmund.

Binstock, Robert H., 1974, "Aging and the Future of American Politics," *The Annals of the American Academy of Political and Social Sciences,* Vol. 415, pp. 199–212.

Birdsall, Stephen S., and J. Michael Gunville, 1977, "The Location of Older Populations in Washington, D.C.: 1940 and 1970," *University of North Carolina Newsletter,* Vol. 62, No. 3, pp. 27–29.

Blenkner, Margaret, 1967, "Environmental Change and the Aging Individual," *Gerontologist* I, Vol. 7, No. 2, pp. 101–105.

Brand, Frederick N., and Richard T. Smith, 1974, "Life Adjustment and Relocation of the Elderly," *Journal of Gerontology,* Vol. 29, No. 3, pp. 336–340.

Brotman, Herman B., 1976, "Every Tenth American—The 'Problem' of Aging," in M. Powell Lawton, Robert J. Newcomer, and Thomas O. Byerts (eds.), *Community Planning for an Aging Society.* Stroudsburg, Pa.: Dowden, Hutchinson & Ross, pp. 5–18.

———, 1977, "Population Projections: Part 1. Tomorrow's Older Population (to 2000)," *Gerontologist,* Vol. 17, No. 3, p. 208.

Brown, Lawrence A., and Eric G. Moore, 1970, "The Intraurban Migration Process: A Perspective," *Geografiska Annaler,* Vol. 52, Series B, pp. 1–13.

Bultena, Gordon L., and Vivian Wood, 1969, "The American Retirement Community: Bane or Blessing?" *Journal of Gerontology,* Vol. 24, No. 2, pp. 209–217.

Burkhardt, Jon E., and Armando M. Lago, 1976, *Methods of Predicting Rural Transit Demand.* Commonwealth of Pennsylvania: Department of Transportation.

Cantilli, Edmund J., and June L. Shmelzer (eds.), 1971, *Transportation and Aging: Selected Issues.* Based on proceedings of the Interdisciplinary Workshop on Transportation and Aging, Washington, D.C., May 24–26, 1970, Washington, D.C.: U.S. Government Printing Office.

Carp, Frances M., 1971, "Public Transit and Retired People," in Edmund J. Cantilli and June L. Shmelzer (eds.), *Transportation and Aging: Selected Issues.* Based on proceedings of the Interdisciplinary Workshop on Transportation and Aging, Washington, D.C., May 24–26, Washington, D.C.: U.S. Government Printing Office, pp. 82–92.

———, 1972, "Retired People as Automobile Passengers," *Gerontologist,* Vol. 12, No. 1, pp. 66–72.

Catau, John C., 1978, "The Role of Distance in the Migration of Retirees to St. Petersburg, Florida," mimeographed. Charlotte: University of North Carolina at Charlotte, Department of Geography and Earth Sciences.

Cebula, Richard J., 1974, "The Quality of Life and Migration of the Elderly," *Review of Regional Studies,* Vol. 4, No. 1, pp. 62–68.

Chevan, Albert, and L. R. Fischer, 1978, "Retirement and Interstate Migration," paper presented at the Annual Meeting of the Population Association of America, Atlanta, Georgia.

Clark, Lorraine H., and Samuel W. Cochran, 1972, "Needs of Older Americans Assessed by Delphi Procedures," *Journal of Gerontology,* Vol. 27, No. 2, pp. 275–278.

Coale, Ansley J., 1964, "How a Population Ages or Grows Younger," in Ronald Freedman (ed.), *Population: The Vital Revolution.* Garden City, N.Y.: Anchor Books, pp. 47–58.

Cowgill, Donald O., 1970, "The Demography of Aging," in Adeline M. Hoffman (ed.), *The Daily Needs and Interests of Older People.* Springfield, Ill.: Thomas, pp. 27–69.

———, and Samuel F. Ostertag, Jr., 1962, *The People of Wichita, 1960.* Wichita, Kans.: The Urban Studies Center.

Cumming, Elaine, and William E. Henry, 1961, *Growing Old: The Process of Disengagement.* New York: Basic Books.

Cutler, Neal E., and John R. Schmidhauser, 1975, "Age and Political Behavior," in Diana S. Woodruff and James E. Birren (eds.), *Aging: Scientific Perspectives and Social Issues.* New York: D. Van Nostrand, pp. 374–406.

———, and Robert A. Harootyan, 1975, "Demography of the Aged," in Diana S. Woodruff and James E. Birren (eds.), *Aging: Scientific Perspectives and Social Issues.* New York: D. Van Nostrand, p. 36.

Flynn, Cynthia B., 1978, "Unusual Interstate Migration Streams—An Application of Transaction Flow Analysis," paper presented at the Annual Meeting of the American Sociological Association, September, San Francisco, California.

Friedsam, Hiram J., and Cora A. Martin, 1973, "Travel by Older People as a Use of Leisure," *Gerontologist,* Vol. 13, No. 2, pp. 204–207.

Garrison, William L., 1971, "Limitations and Constraints of Existing Transportation Systems as Applied to the Elderly," in Edmund J. Cantilli and June L. Shmelzer (eds.), *Transportation and Aging: Selected Issues.* Based on proceedings of the Interdisciplinary Workshop on Transportation and Aging, Washington, D.C., May 24–26, Washington, D.C.: U.S. Government Printing Office, pp. 100–106.

Glenn, Norval D., 1977, *Cohort Analysis,* in E. M. Uslaner (ed.), *Quantitative Applications in Social Science Series.* Beverly Hills, Calif.: Sage.

Golant, Stephen M., 1972, *The Residential Location and Spatial Behavior of the Elderly: A Canadian Example.* Chicago, Ill.: University of Chicago, Department of Geography Research Paper No. 143.

———, 1975, "Residential Concentrations of the Future Elderly," *Gerontologist* II, Vol. 15, No. 1, pp. 16–23.

———, 1976a, "Housing and Transportation Problems of of the Urban Elderly," in John S. Adams (ed.), *Urban Policymaking and Metropolitan Dynamics: A Comparative Geographical Analysis.* Cambridge, Mass.: Ballinger, pp. 379–422.

———, 1976b, "Intraurban Transportation Needs and Problems of the Elderly," in M. Powell Lawton, Robert J. Newcomer, and Thomas O. Byerts (eds.), *Community for an Aging Society.* Stroudsburg, Pa.: Dowden, Hutchinson & Ross, pp. 282–308.

———, 1977, "Spatial Context of Residential Moves by Elderly Persons," *International Journal of Aging and Human Development,* Vol. 8, No. 3, pp. 279–289.

———, 1978, "The Literal Mobilization of Goods and Services for Older People," paper presented at the First National Conference on Community Housing Choices for Older Americans, Philadelphia, Pennsylvania.

Goldscheider, Calvin, 1966, "Differential Residential Mobility of the Older Population," *Journal of Gerontology,* Vol. 21, No. 1, pp. 103–108.

Goldstein, Sidney, 1967, "Socio-Economic and Migration Differentials Between the Aged in the Labor Force and in the Labor Reserve," *Gerontologist,* Vol. 7, No. 1, pp. 31–40, 79.

Graff, Thomas O., and Robert F. Wiseman, 1978, "Changing Concentrations of Older Americans," *The Geographical Review,* Vol. 68, No. 4, pp. 379–393.

Gubrium, Jaber F., 1972, "Toward A Socioenvironmental Theory of Aging," *Gerontologist,* Vol. 12, No. 3, pp. 281–284.

———, 1973, *The Myth of the Golden Years: A Socio-Environmental Theory of Aging.* Springfield, Ill.: Charles C. Thomas.

Hanson, Perry, 1978, "The Activity Patterns of Elderly Households," *Geografiska Annaler,* Vol. 59, Series B, No. 2, pp. 109–124.

Harris, Louis, and Associates, Inc., 1975, *The Myth and Reality of Aging in America.* Washington, D.C.: The National Council on the Aging, Inc.

Hiltner, John, and Bruce W. Smith, 1974a, "Location Patterns of the Urban Elderly: Are They Segregated?" *Great Plains—Rocky Mountain Geographical Journal,* Vol. 3, pp. 43–48.

———, 1974b, "Intraurban Residential Mobility of the Elderly," *Journal of Geography,* Vol. 73, No. 4, pp. 23–33.

Hodge, David, and Susan Schold, 1977, *Elderly Transit Use in Metropolitan Seattle.* Washington, D.C.: U.S. Department of Transportation, Urban Mass Transportation Administration.

Hoover, E. M., and R. Vernon, 1962, *Anatomy of a Metropolis.* Garden City, New York: Doubleday.

Johnston, Ronald J., 1971, *Urban Residential Patterns.* New York: Praeger.

Kahana, Eva, 1975, "A Congruence Model of Person-Environment Interaction," in Paul G. Windley, Thomas O. Byerts, and F. Gene Ernst (eds.), *Theory Development in Environment and Aging.* Washington, D.C.: Gerontological Society, pp. 181–214.

Kennedy, John M., and Gordon F. DeJong, 1977, "Aged in Cities: Residential Segregation in 10 U.S.A. Central Cities," *Journal of Gerontology,* Vol. 32, No. 1, pp. 97–102.

Lawton, M. Powell, and Bonnie Simon, 1968, "The Ecology of Social Relationships in Housing for the Elderly," *Gerontologist,* Vol. 8, No. 2, pp. 108–115.

———, Morton H. Kleban, and Diane A. Carlson, 1973, "The Inner-City Resident: To Move or Not to Move," *Gerontologist,* Vol. 13, No. 4, pp. 443–448.

———, and Lucille Nahemov, 1973, "Ecology and the Aging Process," in Carl Eisdorfer and M. Powell Lawton (eds.), *The Psychology of Adult Development and Aging.* Washington, D.C.: American Psychological Association, pp. 619-674.

———, and Jacob Cohen, 1974, "Environment and the Well-Being of Inner-City Residents," *Environment and Behavior,* Vol. 6, No. 2, pp. 195-211.

———, 1975a, "Competence, Environmental Press, and the Adaptation of Older People," in Paul G. Windley, Thomas O. Byerts, and F. Gene Ernst (eds.), *Theory Development in Environment and Aging.* Washington, D.C.: Gerontological Society, pp. 13–83.

———, Robert J. Newcomer, and Thomas O. Byerts (eds.), 1976, *Community Planning for an Aging Society: Design of Facilities and Services.* Stroudsburg, Pa.: Dowden, Hutchinson & Ross.

Lenzer, Antony, 1965, "Mobility Patterns Among the Aged," *Gerontologist,* Vol. 5, No. 1, pp. 12–15.

Leslie, Gerald R., and Arthur H. Richardson, 1961, "Life-Cycle, Career Pattern, and the Decision to Move," *American Sociological Review,* Vol. 26, No. 6, pp. 894–902.

Manley, Charles R., Jr., 1954, "The Migration of Older People," *American Journal of Sociology,* Vol. 59, No. 4, pp. 324–332.

Manney, James D., Jr., 1975, *Aging in American Society—An Examination of Concepts and Issues.* Ann Arbor, Mich.: University of Michigan, The Institute of Gerontology.

Marble, Duane F., Perry Hanson, and Susan Hanson, 1973, *Household Travel Behavior Study: Intraurban Mobility Patterns of Elderly Households. A Swedish Example.* Proceedings of the International Conference on Transportation Research, May, Bruges, Belgium, pp. 655–664.

Markovitz, Joani K., 1971, "Transportation Needs of the Elderly," *Traffic Quarterly,* Vol. 25, No. 2, pp. 237–253.

Markson, Elizabeth W., Gary S. Levitz, and Maryvonne Gognalons-Caillard, 1973, "The Elderly and the Community: Reidentifying Unmet Needs," *Journal of Gerontology,* Vol. 28, No. 4, pp. 503–509.

McKelvey, Douglas J., 1974, "An Analysis of the Development and Impact of a Rural Public Transportation

System," unpublished paper, Department of Geography, University of Iowa.

———, and Kenneth J. Dueker, 1974, "Transportation Planning: The Urban and Rural Interface and Transit Needs of the Rural Elderly," *Technical Report #26*. Iowa City, Iowa: University of Iowa, Center for Urban Transportation Studies, Institute of Urban and Regional Research.

———, and John A. Lichtenheld, 1975, "Do Elderly Demand-Responsive Systems Duplicate Existing Fixed Route Systems?" *Technical Report #45*. Iowa City, Iowa: University of Iowa, Center for Urban Transportation Studies, Institute of Urban and Regional Research.

———, 1975, "The Rise and Fall of Transportation Demonstrations for the Transportation Disadvantaged," paper presented at the 5th Annual Florida Transportation Conference, "Improving the Quality and Quantity of Transportation," Orlando, Florida.

Michelson, William, 1970, *Man and His Urban Environment: A Sociological Approach*. Reading, Mass.: Addison-Wesley.

Miller, Joel A., 1976, "Latent Travel Demands of the Handicapped and Elderly," in National Research Council, Transportation Research Board, *Transportation Issues: The Disadvantaged, the Elderly, and Citizen Involvement*. Washington, D.C.: National Academy of Sciences, Transportation Research Record 618, pp. 7–12.

Nelson, Linda M., and Mary Winter, 1975, "Life Disruptions, Independence, Satisfaction, and the Consideration of Moving," *Gerontologist*, Vol. 15, No. 2, pp. 160–164.

Neugarten, Bernice L., 1975, "The Future and the Young-Old," *Gerontologist* II, Vol. 15, No. 1, pp. 4–9.

Newcomer, Robert J., 1975, *Group Housing for the Elderly: Defining Neighborhood Service Convenience for Public Housing and Section 202 Residences*. Ph.D. dissertation, University of Southern California, Los Angeles.

Niebanck, Paul L., 1965, *The Elderly in Older Urban Areas: Problems of Adaption and the Effects of Relocation*. Philadelphia, Pa.: University of Pennsylvania, Institute for Environmental Studies.

Orbach, Harold L., 1974, *The Disengagement Theory of Aging 1960–1970. A Case Study of Scientific Controversy*. Ph.D. dissertation, University of Minnesota.

Palmore, Erdman, 1971, "Variables Related to Needs Among the Aged Poor," *Journal of Gerontology*, Vol. 26, No. 4, pp. 524–531.

———, and Frank Whittington, 1971, "Trends in the Relative Status of the Aged," *Social Forces*, Vol. 50, No. 1, pp. 84–91.

Pampel, Fred C., and Harvey M. Choldin, 1978, "Urban Location and Segregation of the Aged: A Block-Level Analysis," *Social Forces*, Vol. 56, No. 4, pp. 1121–1139.

Pastalan, Leon A., 1975, "Research in Environment and Aging: An Alternative to Theory," in Paul G. Windley, Thomas O. Byerts, and F. Gene Ernst (eds.), *Theory Development in Environment and Aging*. Washington, D.C.: Gerontological Society, pp. 219–230.

———, and Daniel H. Carson, 1970, *Spatial Behavior of of Older People*. Ann Arbor, Michigan: University of Michigan, Institute of Gerontology.

Popper, Robert J., Charles B. Notess, and Ricardo N. Zapata, 1976, "Demand for Special Transit Systems to Serve the Rural Elderly," in National Research Council, Transportation Research Board, *Transportation Issues: The Disadvantaged, the Elderly, and Citizen Involvement*. Washington, D.C.: National Academy of Sciences, Transportation Research Record 618, pp. 1–6.

Population Reference Bureau, 1975, "The Elderly in America," *Population Bulletin*, Vol. 30, No. 3, pp. 1–36.

Preston, Valerie, 1978, *Life Cycle Effects on Residential Area Evaluation*. Ph.D. dissertation, McMaster University.

Rapoport, Amos, 1973, "An Approach to the Construction of Man-Environment Theory," in W. F. E. Preiser (ed.), *EDRA Proceedings II*. Stroudsburg, Pa.: Dowden, Hutchinson & Ross, pp. 124–135.

Regnier, Victor, 1974, "Matching Older Persons' Cognition with Their Use of Neighborhood Areas," in D. H. Carson (ed.), *Man-Environment Interactions: Evaluations and Applications, Part III*. Stroudsburg, Pa.: Dowden, Hutchinson & Ross, pp. 19–40.

———, 1976, "Neighborhoods as Service Systems," in M. Powell Lawton, Robert J. Newcomer, and Thomas O. Byerts (eds.), *Community Planning for an Aging Society*. Stroudsburg, Pa.: Dowden, Hutchinson, & Ross, pp. 240–257.

Roseman, Curtis C., 1977, *Changing Migration Patterns Within the United States*. Washington, D.C.: Association of American Geographers, AAG Resource Paper No. 77-2.

Rossi, Peter H., 1955, *Why Families Move: A Study in the Social Psychology of Urban Residential Mobility*. Glencoe, Ill.: The Free Press.

Rowles, Graham D., 1978, *Prisoners of Space? Exploring the Geographical Experience of Older People*. Boulder, Colo.: Westview Press.

Rushton, Gerard, Michael F. Goodchild, and Lawrence M. Ostresh, Jr., 1973, *Computer Programs for Location-Allocation Problems*. Iowa City, Iowa: University of Iowa, Department of Geography, Monograph Number 6.

Schaie, K. Warner, 1965, "A General Model for the Study of Developmental Problems," *Psychological Bulletin*, Vol. 64, No. 2, pp. 92–107.

Serow, William J., 1978, "Return Migration of the Elderly in the U.S.A.: 1955–1960 and 1965–1970," *Journal of Gerontology*, Vol. 33, No. 2, pp. 288–295.

Shelley, Fred M., 1978, "Search Behavior and Place Utility of Recent Migrants to the Arkansas Ozarks," *Canadian Studies in Population*. (forthcoming).

Shock, Nathan W., 1962, "The Physiology of Aging," *Scientific American*, Vol. 206, pp. 100–110.

Smith, Bruce W., and John Hiltner, 1975, "Intraurban Location of the Elderly," *Journal of Gerontology*, Vol. 30, No. 4, pp. 473–478.

Speare, Alden, Jr., Sidney Goldstein, and William H. Frey, 1974, *Residential Mobility, Migration, and Metropolitan Change*. Cambridge, Mass.: Ballinger.

Sussman, Marvin B., 1976, "The Family Life of Old People," in Robert Binstock and Ethel Shanas (eds.), *Handbook of Aging and the Social Sciences*. New York: Van Nostrand Reinhold, pp. 219–220.

Svart, Larry M., 1976, "Environmental Preference Migration: A Review," *Geographical Review*, Vol. 66, No. 3, pp. 314–330.

Taietz, Philip, 1975, "Community Complexity and Knowledge of Facilities," *Journal of Gerontology*, Vol. 30, No. 3, pp. 357–362.

Tobin, Sheldon S., and Morton A. Lieberman, 1976, *Last Home for the Aged*. San Francisco: Jossey-Bass.

Toffler, Alvin, 1970, *Future Shock*. New York: Random House.

U.S. Bureau of the Census, 1976a (May), *Current Population Reports, Special Studies, Demographic Aspects of Aging and the Older Population in the United States.* Washington, D.C.: U.S. Government Printing Office, Series P-23, No. 59.

U.S. Department of Health, Education, and Welfare, 1975, *Transportation for the Elderly: The State of the Art.* Washington, D.C.: Department of Health, Education, and Welfare, Office of Human Development, Administration on Aging, DHEW Publication No. (OHD) 75-20081.

Van Arsdol, Maurice D., Jr., George S. Sabagh, and Edgar W. Butler, 1968, "Retrospective and Subsequent Metropolitan Residential Mobility," *Demography,* Vol. 5, No. 1, pp. 249-267.

Virden, Mark A., 1976, *Elderly Migratory Behavior in Kansas City, Kansas: Implications for Life Cycle Theory.* Master's thesis, University of Kansas, Department of Geography.

Walker, James, and Karl Price, 1975, "Retirement Choice and Retirement Satisfaction," *Gerontologist* II, Vol. 15, No. 5, p. 50.

Wiseman, Robert F., 1976, "Impact of a Demand-Responsive Mini-Bus Transportation System for the Elderly in a Small Urban Community," *Southeastern Geographer,* Vol. XVI, No. 1, pp. 47-61.

_____, and Mark A. Virden, 1977, "Spatial and Social Dimensions of Intraurban Elderly Migration," *Economic Geography,* Vol. 53, No. 1, pp. 1-13.

_____, and Curtis C. Roseman, 1979, "A Typology of Elderly Migration Based on the Decision Making Process," unpublished paper, Department of Geography, University of Kansas.

_____, and Tim Peterson, "Elderly Intraurban Migration and Independence Loss," *East Lakes Geographer* (forthcoming).

_____, "National Patterns of Elderly Concentration and Migration," in Stephen M. Golant (ed.), *The Locational and Environmental Context of the Elderly Population.* New York: Halsted Press (forthcoming).

Wynn, F. Houston, and Herbert S. Levinson, 1967, "Some Considerations in Appraising Bus Transit Potentials," *Highway Research Board Record,* No. 197, pp. 1-24.

Yee, William, and Maurice D. Van Ardsol, Jr., 1977, Residential Mobility, Age, and the Life Cycle," *Journal of Gerontology,* Vol. 32, No. 2, pp. 211-221.

Further Readings

Barry, John R., and C. Ray Wingrove (eds.), 1977, *Let's Learn About Aging: A Book of Readings.* Cambridge, Mass.: Schenkman.

Bell, Duran, Patricia Kasschau, and Gail Zellman, 1976, *Delivering Services to Elderly Members of Minority Groups: A Critical Review of the Literature.* Santa Monica, Calif.: Rand Paper No. R-1862-HEW.

Beyer, Glenn H., and Margaret E. Woods, 1963, *Living & Activity Patterns of the Aged.* Ithaca, N.Y.: Center for Housing and Environmental Studies, Cornell University.

Brail, Richard K., James W. Hughes, and Carol A. Arthur, 1976, *Transportation Services for the Disabled and Elderly.* New Brunswick, N.J.: Rutgers—The State University of New Jersey, Center for Urban Policy Research.

Chevan, Albert, and John F. O'Rourke, 1972, "Aging Regions of the United States," *Journal of Gerontology,* Vol. 27, No. 1, pp. 119-126.

Cowgill, Donald O., 1978, "Residential Segregation by Age in American Metropolitan Areas," *Journal of Gerontology,* Vol. 33, No. 3, pp. 446-453.

Golant, Stephen, and Rosemary McCaslin, 1978, "A Functional Classification of Services for Older People," paper presented at the National Meeting of the Association of American Geographers, New Orleans, Louisiana.

Gorman, Gilbert, and Jarir S. Dajani, 1975, "Measuring the Performance of Transit Service," Chapel Hill, N.C.: University of North Carolina, Working Paper No. 5, Transit Evaluation Project, Department of City and Regional Planning.

Heintz, Katherine M., 1976, *Retirement Communities.* New Brunswick, N.J.: Rutgers—The State University of New Jersey, Center for Urban Policy Research.

Hood, Thomas C., Thomas L. Bell, and Kenneth W. Heathington, 1978, "Planning for the Transportation Disadvantaged: A Classification of User Groups," paper presented at the International Conference on Transport for Elderly and Handicapped Persons, Cambridge, Mass., Paper No. V-A.

Kart, Cary S., and Barbara B. Manard, 1976, *Aging in America: Readings in Social Gerontology.* Port Washington, N.Y.: Alfred.

Keebler, Nancy (ed.), 1978, *A Guide to Organizations, Agencies, and Federal Programs for Older Americans.* Washington, D.C.: *Older American Reports.*

Lawton, M. Powell, 1975b, *Planning and Managing Housing for the Elderly.* New York: John Wiley & Sons.

National Council on the Aging, 1977, *Publications List.* Washington, D.C.: National Council on the Aging, Inc.

Osterbind, Carter C. (ed.), 1973, *Areawide Planning for Independent Living for Older People.* Gainesville, Fla.: University of Florida Press, Center for Gerontological Studies and Programs.

_____, 1975, *Social Goals, Social Programs and the Aging.* Gainesville, Fla.: University of Florida Press, Center for Gerontological Studies and Programs.

Peet, R., and G. Rowles, 1974, "Social Geography," *Geographical Review,* Vol. 64, No. 2, pp. 287-289.

Stutz, Frederick P., 1977, *Social Aspects of Interaction and Transportation.* Washington, D.C.: Association of American Geographers, Resource Paper No. 76-2.

U.S. Bureau of the Census, 1976b, *U.S. Department of Commerce, Historical Statistics of the United States.* Washington, D.C.: U.S. Government Printing Office.

U.S. Bureau of the Census, 1977, *Current Population Reports, Gross Migration by County: 1965 to 1970.* Washington, D.C.: U.S. Government Printing Office, Series P-25, No. 701.

U.S. Bureau of the Census, 1977, *Current Population Reports, Population Characteristics, Geographical Mobility: March 1975 to March 1976.* Washington, D.C.: U.S. Government Printing Office, Series P-20, No. 305.

U.S. Department of Health, Education, and Welfare, 1976, *The Elderly Population: Estimates by County, 1976.*

Washington, D.C.: Department of Health, Education, and Welfare, Office of Human Development Services—Administration on Aging, National Clearinghouse on Aging, DHEW Publication No. (OHDS) 78–20248.

Wachs, Martin, and Robert D. Blanchard, 1975, *Life Styles and Transportation Needs of the Elderly in the Future*. Springfield, Va.: National Technical Information Service, U.S. Department of Commerce.

Yeates, Maurice, 1978, "The Urban Requirements of Canada's Future Elderly," paper presented at the National Meeting of the Association of American Geographers, New Orleans, Louisiana.